Garden in a Teacup

MINIATURE
INDOOR LANDSCAPING

BY *Carla Wallach*

A HARVEST/HBJ BOOK

HARCOURT BRACE JOVANOVICH

NEW YORK AND LONDON

Printed in the United States of America

Library of Congress Cataloging in Publication Data

Wallach, Magdalena.
Garden in a teacup.

Bibliography: p.
Includes index.
1.   Gardens, Miniature.   2.   Miniature plants.
I.   Title.
SB419.W22   635.9′65   77-12257

ISBN 0-15-634565-X
(paper)
First edition
B C D E

To *Karen Killilea*, with love.
I am blessed to have her as a friend.

Contents

Experience has always been the best teacher and never more so than in gardening. Every dish garden illustrated in this book (and many more not shown for lack of space) was designed, planted, and grown by me. I started doing this in order to gain the necessary experience to pass along to my readers but ended up planting everything in sight for the sheer fun of it. I learned much by doing over one hundred of these miniature gardens. Oddly enough, the ones I thought might be the most difficult turned out to be just the opposite, while others that I expected would be a breeze became disasters. I've obviously not recommended those. Many of the illustrated gardens are now over two or three years old and have flowered many times (but seldom when the photographer came, naturally!). Some plants have changed little with time; others have. Where this occurred, I have described in the captions *how* they changed, together with whatever steps I took to keep them the desired size.

THE DRAWINGS BY LINDA HARRIS ARE BASED ON PHOTOGRAPHS BY LYNNE G. LISCEK.

Introduction

Think small! Be a child again! Gardening with miniature plants is fun because it offers adults the opportunity to indulge the child that dwells within everyone, providing an excuse for playing with doll-sized objects once again.

Planting a miniature garden is probably the most creative form of gardening, yet it requires so little work that a child, a bedridden person, or a gardener afflicted with arthritic hands can handle it with confidence. There are so many varieties of plants available in dwarf form that the gardener can create different moods and various scenes, imitating the foliage of a woodland, a desert, or a lush tropical island.

Selecting the container is a job for the unbridled imagination. Anything goes, as long as it's tiny: an ashtray, a soap dish, a seashell, a champagne glass, a thimble, a teacup, a ladle, a soup plate. The challenge is not to go out and buy a container unless absolutely necessary. Look around the home, especially the kitchen, and visualize an egg cup as a smashing decorative accent when filled with appropriate plants.

Working with miniature gardens is easy because the gardener is in full control of the situation. For one thing, the indoor landscaper does not have to fight nature and the elements, as the outdoor gardener does. Even indoors, a garden of normal-sized house plants can mean a lot of work: grooming, carting plants back and forth to the kitchen sink for washing, carrying heavy watering cans. But the miniature garden is a tiny world, requiring only a few inches of space, several drops of water, and a handful of soil. Just remember that however little water these plants need, they need it more frequently than do their larger counterparts. For this reason, the tiniest of pots, such as a demitasse or an egg cup, are best planted with cacti and succulents, since they can withstand long dry spells.

Lifting the miniature garden from one room to another for a change of scenery will not bring on a backache. And the cost is negligible. The containers are free if the gardener is imaginative, and the amount of soil and fertilizer needed is Lilliputian, which leaves only the cost of the plants themselves.

Even the plants can be free, if taken from cuttings of standard-sized plants. Most cuttings will remain small for a long time if their roots are restricted. And the very young plants available in supermarkets, dime stores, and plant shops are inexpensive because they're so tiny, just a step past the seedling stage. They will take a year or two to outgrow their allotted space. Last but most important are the real miniatures. They're available from mail-order nurseries (see list on pages 131–35) and cost more but are well worth it. To see a perfect, tiny replica of a rose or a geranium is as exciting as staring in wonder at the made-to-scale miniature reproductions of antiques in a dollhouse. As the indoor gardener gains experience in creating dish gardens—inevitably with successful results—the additional expense of buying dwarf plants seems negligible.

An important advantage of mini-gardening is that it doesn't require a room drenched with sunlight to keep the plants alive and healthy. Several inches of sunlight on a window sill, or a corner table that gets bright light for a few hours a day is enough. A half dozen miniature plants can fit in an area that might hold only one standard-sized house plant. The gardener can satisfy the desire for a collection without sacrificing precious space.

It seems that everyone craves the companionship of living things, which explains the tremendous popularity of house plants, but some indoor gardeners simply don't have enough time or enough mobility—due to health—to care for them. A miniature garden is within everyone's capability.

The beginner should be warned, however, that planting miniature gardens is like eating peanuts: it's tough to keep one's enthusiasm under control. It's such fun selecting containers (after a while *everything* small that's lying around the house empty is snapped up and planted) that the collection grows and grows. At this point, the gardener is growing

15

miniatures not because of their practical virtues but simply because they are a beautiful world unto themselves. In this, miniature landscaping is like collecting dollhouses, toy soldiers, miniature furniture, or seashells.

Any good-sized, firm log makes a wonderful container when it's hollowed out for plants. From left to right: Malpighia coccigera and Polystichum tsus simense. Trailing at the base of the miniature daffodils is Selaginella kraussiana (denticulata).

1.

Creative
Containers

I bought this plastic bird feeder (which had a dome cover) with great hopes of attracting birds, except that it somehow didn't work out. However, as a planter it turned into a smashing hanging basket! The center is planted with a clump of Dudleya attenuata "orcuttii" on the left, with a large cluster of Chamaecereus "Hummel's silvestri hybrid." White sand covers the surface. Peeking out of the left hole is Echeveria pallida, while Crassula orbicularis fills the hole on the right. Not shown is a third hole with Sedum dasyphyllum.

Anything goes—only the imagination of the gardener and the size of the plant's root ball limit what can be used as a container. Because the container plays such an important part in the overall design of a miniature garden, it is usually selected before the plants. You can always buy the plants, but to save money you will probably want to choose the containers from whatever happens to be around your home.

Before reaching for the first available teacup or wine glass, stop and consider your objective. Do you want one tiny plant to decorate the corner of an end table? Or are you planning the miniature garden as focal point of a dining room or coffee table? Perhaps you'd like a collection of small plants that can be grouped attractively on a glass shelf across a window. If you've quit smoking, you may be thinking that your handsome crystal ashtray would look great on your desk holding a few cacti.

Containers convey a mood and a style. This should be considered when making a selection. Where you plan to locate your micro-garden also affects the selection of a container. A pewter soup ladle holding a small plant is at home hanging against a wall or lying on a window sill in the kitchen or dining room. The same is true of other kitchen utensils and everyday dishes. But brandy snifters, stemmed glasses, driftwood, and ceramic dishes are more suitable with living room furnishings.

If you have a collection of dollhouse dishes, thimbles, shells, measuring cups, or a few crystal glasses that are chipped and no longer used, you have the makings of a unique decorative accent (if it shows, hide the chip with a plant cascading over the edge). Five or six coffee mugs, each with its own plant, grouped on a large platter make a statement, as decorators say. If you have old inkwells and never knew how to display them, fill each with a plant and place them in a row on a flat desk-table or a bookshelf (with a strip of artificial lighting above them unless the shelf gets good light).

It's difficult to say how deep the container should

When I found this empty bird's nest outside my greenhouse door, I couldn't resist planting it. I first lined it with plastic wrap in which I had made a few holes with a toothpick, then planted it with a young seedling of Malpighia coccigera and Pilea microphylla (muscosa). After a year or so, the nest began falling apart, but it certainly was a conversation piece for a long time!

Large shells are great for bromeliads such as this
Hechtia tillandsioides teamed with burro's tail,
Sedum morganianum. The smaller shell, only
slightly larger than a golf ball, is shown on top of
a sand paperweight and planted with the miniature begonia "China Doll." The doll obviously
likes her home because it's now in its third year.

I always thought these Italian copper measuring cups were far too beautiful to use, so I planted them. From left: Aeonium haworthii, Aloe humilis "globosa," Aeonium canariense, Mammillaria "dolichocentra," Mammillaria columbiana, Mammillaria geminispina. I keep these out of direct sunlight because even though I purposely kept within the cactus family, metal containers heat quickly in sunlight.

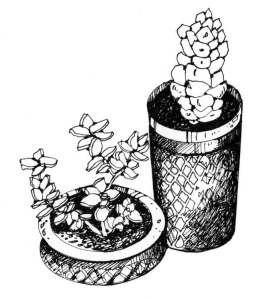

Individual ashtray-and-cigarette-holder sets are seldom seen anymore on dinner party tables. Bring one out of hiding and plant it. The ashtray is filled with Crassula socialis, while the cigarette shows off Crassula cordata.

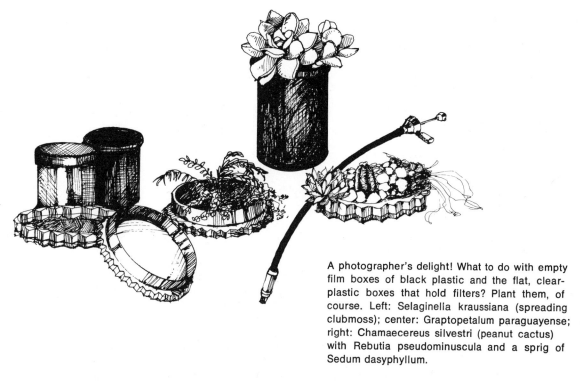

A photographer's delight! What to do with empty film boxes of black plastic and the flat, clear-plastic boxes that hold filters? Plant them, of course. Left: Selaginella kraussiana (spreading clubmoss); center: Graptopetalum paraguayense; right: Chamaecereus silvestri (peanut cactus) with Rebutia pseudominuscula and a sprig of Sedum dasyphyllum.

If only my grandmother could see what happened to her pressed-glass divided salt-and-pepper dish! It's no taller than a golf ball and about twice the width. On the left side I stuck a few peanut cacti, Chamaecereus silvestri, plucked from a mother plant, together with Crassula pseudolycopodioides; on the right: Crassula lycopodioides.

be because it all depends on the plants. One thing is sure, however: it should be large enough to hold the root ball of the plant. If the plant becomes potbound, it will stop growing but will continue to live happily. Small containers are one way to keep small plants small. A tiny seedling planted properly will grow to its full height but if contained within a tiny area will stay small for a long time.

There is nothing to stop you from buying a container, but before you do, consider the endless variety available around you:

any shallow dish or bowl
plastic or Plexiglas containers
cereal bowls
ashtrays
glass, metal, or heavy aluminum foil baking pans (spray paint them a flat black)
thimbles
teacups
small brandy snifters
stemmed glasses of all sizes
cocktail glasses
molds
wicker and straw baskets with saucers or aluminum foil as liners
dollhouse dishes
candy jars
kitchen containers
ladles
small ceramic dishes in all shapes and colors
soup plates
individual wine decanters
small glass or plastic cloche on a plate makes a terrarium
animal-shaped clay pots
bonsai pots
salt cellars
shells
porous rocks or featherrock
inkwells
custard cups
soap dishes
individual salad bowls
any dish with tiny feet
small glass canning jars
fish tank or large brandy snifter as "greenhouse" for several plants
soufflé dishes
metal desk "organizers" (round cylinders of different heights glued together)
cosmetic jars

Oriental shops, variety stores, and hardware departments are the best places for scouting around if you simply can't find a suitable container at home. One word of caution: when considering a container,

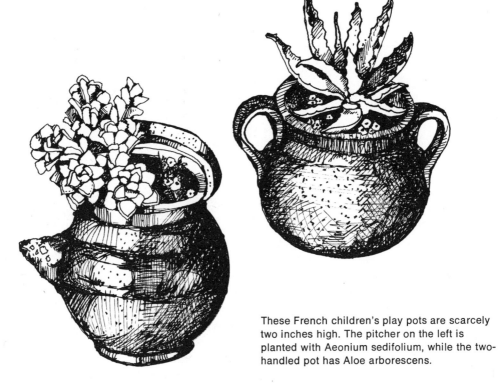

These French children's play pots are scarcely two inches high. The pitcher on the left is planted with Aeonium sedifolium, while the two-handled pot has Aloe arborescens.

picture it with plants in it. A ceramic dish with an ornate design distracts the eye from the plants. An exception can be made if you intend to show off only one plant in a pot and the plant is a nonflowering one.

Since most miniature gardens are displayed on furniture, check to see if the container is totally waterproof (unglazed clay, for example, is not). In such a case, use a glass, a plastic pan, or extra-strength aluminum foil as a liner inside the pot.

The ideal container has holes in the bottom so that water can drain out properly. But only pots manufactured specifically for plants have such drainage holes. The creative miniature gardener is naturally drawn to unusual containers that were originally meant to perform quite other functions and have no such holes. Double potting is recommended with standard-sized house plants, but in the case of tiny containers it's obviously impossible to put plant, pot, and all inside a sherry glass. Planting directly into the container is the usual procedure. The risk of overwatering can be kept under control far more easily in tiny containers, since only a few drops are needed at a time. (See Chapter 8 for details on watering.)

The smaller the container, the more sense it makes to plant it with cacti or succulents. These require very little water, and since water evaporates so rapidly in tiny pots, the plants won't be injured if the soil goes dry for a while. Not so with other plants, so larger containers (by miniature standards) should be selected for more elaborate landscape scenes such as a woodland. A baking pan is ideal for the latter. I did a woodland scene (see page 53 for illustration) in a disposable aluminum pan painted black and inserted in a wicker tray, and the plants have been thriving for a long time.

Sometimes one is amazed at how nature adapts so readily to what might be called trying situations. Four years ago I planted a hairy cactus inside a shell that is open at both ends. It created a kind of spiral effect and was quite dramatic looking but unable to hold more than a few grains of soil. The cactus is doing beautifully, even growing. Another surprise involved a much smaller shell, in which I planted a miniature begonia (see page 21 for illustration). The soil—what there is of it—dries out very quickly, but to my amazement the tiny begonia is happily growing. These are exceptions, I realize, but I mention them so that you don't get too uptight about so-called rules.

2.

Gardens
in Soil

An antique tole cream pitcher is a handsome
container for a miniature African violet. This
beauty is Saintpaulia shumensis, but there are
dozens more to choose from.

You've decided where the miniature garden will be displayed, and you've selected the container. To decide what to put in it you must again consider your objective. Is it to show off one plant? To group several plants in one container? To have a mini-landscape with a theme, such as a woodland scene? To highlight a small piece of sculpture, a pretty stone picked up at the beach?

The size and style of the container will determine to a large degree the kind of planting it will take. Let's consider each type separately.

One-Plant Gardens

Let's say your container is a champagne glass or a ceramic mug and you've decided you want just one plant in it. Whatever plant you select, keep in mind the scale of the plant to the container. A heavy-looking plant, even if it has the tiniest root ball, is out of place in a delicate container such as a brandy glass or a shell and would cause it to topple over. A cactus needs room around it to look its best. Midget African violets or sinningias, on the other hand, can take up all the available space in the container and never appear ungraceful. The plant should look important in the container, not be overpowered by it.

If the container is minute, such as a thimble or an egg cup, you can dispense with a layer of drainage material since there won't be room for it and the soil as well. Water evaporates very quickly in such Lilliputian pots, so the risk of overwatering—a proper fear in every good gardener's heart—is virtually nonexistent if care is taken to water correctly (see Chapter 8, on watering).

In the case of larger containers such as a salad bowl or a soufflé dish, it's absolutely necessary to provide good drainage. If the container is transparent, use clean gravel for appearance's sake. Otherwise, broken shard (small broken bits of clay pots) will do nicely. Whenever you're planting directly into

Miniature geraniums are just as prolific bloomers as their larger counterparts. This one, "Jaunty Strawberry Red," looks right at home in a coffee cup.

a container without holes, be as generous as possible with the drainage material, while still leaving room for the soil and root ball. Add small charcoal bits before adding the soil, to keep it sweet smelling. Tap the top of the old pot gently, and very slowly take out the plant. Shake off excess soil from the roots without damaging them only if the new container is too small to hold the root ball intact. Place the plant in the new container, and add a tiny bit of soil around it, pressing down gingerly with your fingers or, better still, with the rubber tip of a pencil or a Q-tip. Water sparingly, using an eyedropper if the pot is very small.

An easy way of potting a tiny plant is to moisten the root ball and the soil to be added before planting. Only a few drops of water are then needed after planting to settle the soil. Placing pieces of damp moss (sphagnum or green sheet moss) on the surface keeps the soil cool and prevents it from drying out too quickly. But don't do this with cacti or succulents. Instead, use perlite, fine gravel, or sand as a surface mulch.

Try a trailing plant if your container has a tall stem. It will cascade gracefully down the sides and will be shown to best advantage. Other plants, while not exactly trailers, nevertheless have a drooping habit that also lends itself to stemmed containers.

Multiple-Plant Gardens

Combining two or more plants in a container creates a charming scene. Scale is important, and so are the form of the plant and the texture of the leaves. Have one plant taller than the rest to create a focal point, with lower plants alongside. In a stemmed container or one with feet, the addition of a hanging plant or one allowed to spill over the edge adds further interest. A ground-cover plant such as selaginella sets off a special specimen plant, forming a carpet of green at its feet and unifying the design. Tiny peb-

What better container for dainty miniature roses than a fragile china teacup. These tiny but perfectly formed flowers are no bigger than one inch across. "Dresden Doll" is shown here, but many others are available.

Exotic orchids are far easier to grow indoors than
most people suspect, especially cymbediums.
Pictured in a tiny wooden slatted pot is a
miniature cymbedium, showing off its spray of
delicate flowers.

I wanted a freeform container, so I made it myself with packaged clay bought at a hobby shop. It was my first attempt at modeling clay, and was I proud when I did it in half an hour! Haworthia fasciata at the left, with trailing Crassula perfossa. A covering of perlite unifies the design and sets the plants off from the container.

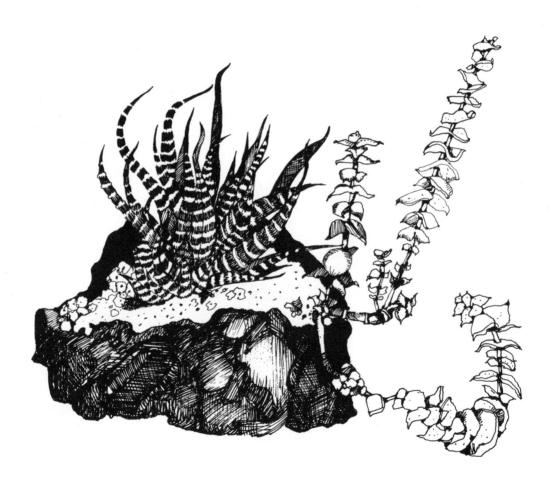

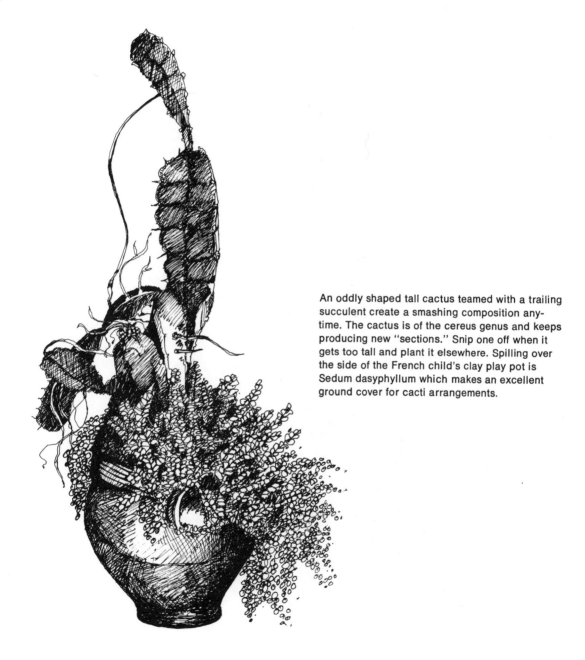

An oddly shaped tall cactus teamed with a trailing succulent create a smashing composition anytime. The cactus is of the cereus genus and keeps producing new "sections." Snip one off when it gets too tall and plant it elsewhere. Spilling over the side of the French child's clay play pot is Sedum dasyphyllum which makes an excellent ground cover for cacti arrangements.

bles, sand, or green sheet moss also make good mulches that act as ground covers.

The most important thing to remember in combining plants is to select those of similar cultural requirements. Plants that require a lot of moisture won't make it alongside those that like it dry. One of them will die. Cacti and succulents are frequently seen together because they share the same needs. Ferns and mosses are compatible. Flowering plants require sun, while foliage plants settle for less light. Plants that like high humidity, such as sinningias or Venus fly-traps, are best used in brandy snifters or glass containers with small openings. You can cover these completely with glass and call them terrariums. Or if you wish, leave these humidity-loving plants in attractive, clean pots with drainage holes and display them inside a large brandy snifter or a fish tank. Make a bed of pebbles or layers of colored sand, and place the pots on top. Then you can change the plants as you wish, varying the design to suit your wishes. Place plants that like it dry on a shallow container with an inch of pebbles or perlite.

When in doubt as to which plants share similar culture requirements, stick to the same family of plants. You can still have variety in your composition. Three or four begonias or geraniums or a few ferns make attractive dish gardens, yet because of different varieties in each family you need not worry about monotony. With flowering plants, try to have at least one with white flowers. If the others in the same dish are pink, lavender, and red, for example, the white acts as a good divider of colors that might otherwise clash and also adds a cooling element to the design. The touch of white is equally effective when used alone with foliage plants. You can't go wrong if you combine colors that are in the same general category. For example, light pinks, deep pinks, and lavenders look well together, as do pale peach and deep orange.

If the container is large enough, you can keep plants in their pots if you so desire and bury the pots in a mulch of pebbles or perlite or moss. This takes

An 8½″, round, unglazed bonsai container holds a variety of delightful and easy-to-get plants. In the background are graceful branches of Malpighia coccigera which resembles miniature holly. At its base are Polygonum (knotweed), Pilea involucrata, and Euonymus japonica microphyllus variegatus. A carpet of Helxine soleiroli (Baby's Tears) holds the design together. Periodic cutting back of the Malpighia and Polygonum is necessary.

An ordinary ceramic eggcup is home to the exotic Monvillea cavendishii, with the ever-graceful Sedum dasyphyllum covering the surface and cascading down the front.

up considerably more room, however, and limits the arrangements you can make.

Keep scale in mind whenever you buy plants for a specific container. The plants shouldn't look lost in the dish. Since their roots are restricted from further growth by the small space, what you buy is pretty much what you'll see for a good time to come so select plants that have reached the size you need right now. A bit of pruning later on will keep them within bounds. The size of a plant's root ball can be deceptive. Begonias, for example, have tiny root balls compared to the size of the plant, while the opposite is true of most ferns. So keep the depth of your container in mind while shopping for plants to fill it.

You can create a mood with several plants, without going in for realistic scenery. Using a basket as a container, take a piece of driftwood or any weathered wood, surround it with ferns and mosses, and you have a charming mini-garden (line the basket with a glass or foil pie plate or extra-heavy aluminum foil). Plant three or four cacti in a low clay dish, add a stone or two with interesting shapes and a top layer of perlite or white sand, and yet another mood is obtained.

When combining several plants in one container, leaf texture and color are important points to consider. There are so many shades of green in foliage—not to mention variegated plants—that it's easy for the gardener to add color contrast and leaf variety to a tiny landscape. Growth habits also contribute interest to the design. Some plants grow tall and skinny, while others are squat and short. Group the plants on a newspaper before planting, switching them around until you are satisfied with what goes next to what for maximum effect. Then plant them the same way. When buying plants, do the same thing at the store. It's a quick way of noticing glaring mistakes in time to avoid them.

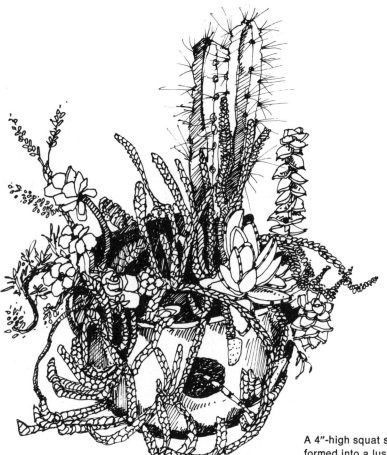

A 4"-high squat strawberry jar is quickly trans-
formed into a lush desert garden. Dominating the
scene are two tall cacti, Cereus peruvianus, with
spikes of Crassula lycopodioides growing straight
up in front of them and sprawling all over the
rest of the container, curving upward as they
reach bottom. To the right of the cacti, growing
out of a hole, is Crassula perfossa. The large,
fleshy leaves of Kalanchoe tomentosa near the
center make a good contrast. Aeonium haworthii
grows out of the center hole, and Echeveria
glauca with its golden yellow flower sprays fills
a hole to the left.

The tiniest strawberry jar, less than twice the height of a golf ball, is the perfect container for the dwarf begonia "Lillian Jarrett" shown here in bloom. In the left opening is a tiny Begonia "Foliosa" which has a drooping habit. The center shows off the miniature Begonia "Dew Drop," and to the right is the miniature Begonia "Baby Rainbow." A delightful way to display a collection of miniature begonias.

Landscaped Gardens

A landscaped garden differs from a multiple-plant garden in that it tells a story or re-creates a natural scene. Adding miniature accessories such as animals, people, bridges, houses, and Oriental temples helps mini-gardeners be as realistic as they wish. You can create a scene from childhood or a favorite vacation spot. Imagination is the key factor. Don't all children love playing with barnyard toys, re-arranging the animals to indicate whether they are on their way back to the barn at the end of the day or grazing peacefully in the meadow? We never really lose our desire to play with toys. We call it "working with miniatures" when we become adults, but we're still playing out our fantasies.

The important thing to remember when selecting plants for various garden motifs is that they should look like those generally found in a real setting. For example, when doing a forest landscape, don't use cacti, dracaenas, or palms. It's by no means necessary to stick only with plants found in the woods, but whatever plant material is used should give the impression that it could be found there. If a tropical plant is a look-alike for a woodland one, it's fine to add it to the landscape. You're striving for the *illusion* of a scene. Later, if you become a purist after planting several successful miniature gardens, you can always strictly limit yourself to what would be actually found in the locale you are reproducing on a tiny scale. A few cows or sheep and some geese and chickens will create a farm scene nicely. Similarly, just one *torii* (archway) or temple or lantern will convey an Oriental mood if teamed with appropriate plants. You can also try a sailboat on a lake, a jungle with a lion, a forest with deer, an oasis surrounded by the desert. The list is endless.

If you are fortunate to come across a variety of miniature accessories, tastefully designed and in scale with one another, you can create a whole New England or Swiss village or a cattle ranch. But re-

Animal planters are all the rage, whether in glazed ceramic or unglazed red clay such as the 6"-high illustrated "baby fish." The Crassula rosularis in bloom has multiplied its rosettes over the last few years, spreading slowly but steadily. On the other hand, the Ceropegia woodii vine has scarcely grown.

straint in the use of accessories is necessary in achieving a proper balance.

All landscaped gardens start the same way: with a container, a liner if the latter is not waterproof (use sturdy plastic, double-strength aluminum foil, or a shallow pan), a layer of finely broken shard, or gravel for drainage, and, finally, soil. Select plants that share the same soil, light, and water requirements. Most are quite happy with an all-purpose soil mixture, but for plants that need extra lime or acidity, it's too difficult to provide them with their own special soil if they are grouped with other plants in a small dish.

Much of the pleasure in creating miniature gardens is derived from working with genuine dwarf plants. Many are now available but must usually be purchased from mail-order houses specializing in miniature plants. But these can be costly, depending on how many are needed. I suggest that the beginner first acquire experience by working with seedlings of standard-sized varieties. Friends will gladly give you cuttings of their plants, which you can root in water or damp vermiculite. To illustrate this point, I have purposely designed many of the miniature gardens illustrated in this book around small-leaved varieties of ordinary house plants, inserting a real miniature here and there. This involves little money but a good deal more pruning to keep the plants within desired height and width.

There are always a few failures at first, until you get the hang of it. Experiment with inexpensive, readily available house plants; then send for the rarer dwarf varieties. These miniatures are exquisite, doll-sized replicas of their larger cousins. They're great fun to work with and well worth the extra effort and money. (See List of Suppliers on page 129.)

It's not easy to find accessories that are tiny enough to be roughly in scale with dwarf plants. You can't have a chicken half the height of the tree towering over it, although poetic license is a must. Again, it's the illusion that matters. If when it's finished, the landscape looks right to your eye, with nothing jarring it, you've succeeded. Best sources for

The movie *Swept Away* inspired me to do this tropical island scene. The large hunk of featherock has dwarf palms on either side (Chamaedorea elegans "bella" or C. elegans "Collinia") with a Screw Pine seedling (Pandanus pygmaeus). To the right is the exotic Kalanchoe fedtschenkoi "marginata," while to the left foreground is Peperomia acuminata. Brown stones serve as "boulders" at the base of the volcanic rock "mountain." Smooth white stone, then gravel, and finally white sand form the beach front. A few pieces of coral finish the scene. A small wicker basket lined with plastic and filled with soil holds your dream island in the sun.

miniature accessories are dealers in miniature furniture, terrarium specialists, variety stores (especially at Christmas time), and special Christmas sales held by garden clubs and garden centers. Many of these miniatures are used to make wreaths and decorations for the holidays, so they are a good time to shop. Of course, making accessories yourself out of baker's clay or some other material will introduce you to a brand-new hobby. There are plenty of books available in the arts-and-crafts field for those who are interested.

The Barnyard Garden. You'll need a few farm animals (choose from cows, sheep, horses, chickens, rabbits, pigs, ducks), a barn in scale with the size of the animals, and a meadow. A farmhouse with a fenced-in courtyard is another possibility. The barn and house can be made out of heavy cardboard, the first painted the usual barnyard red and the latter white with black shutters. Use wooden toothpicks glued together to make a split-rail fence; a picket fence can be simulated by cut-out white plastic plant labels. Use waterproof adhesive to glue the parts together. A farmer and/or his wife can be used instead of buildings. Lawn grass seed makes a fine meadow, which is kept "mowed" with manicuring scissors. Add a few "trees" (carissa, small-leaved ivy, euonymus, evergreen seedlings). A small clump of dried baby's-tears looks like fruit trees in bloom or, if tinted green, like a grove of small trees. Remove the lower leaves of the plant to give the tree its trunk, except with evergreens. For "shrubs," use peperomias or pileas to name just two, either bought young or in dwarf varieties. Sow a few seeds of the coarser rye grass to fill out the landscape, giving it a natural look when trimmed unevenly.

Don't incorporate all your ideas in one garden. Keep the design simple. Let the rolling meadow be the focal point with animals and a barn. Or focus on the farmhouse and courtyard. Which you choose depends on the kinds of animals you have. Sheep, cattle, and horses look best in the meadow. Chicken,

A fun indoor garden for a child to make: a Bavarian village nestled at the foot of a snow-capped mountain. I bought the imported hand-made, brightly colored wooden toy set from a mail-order firm. The church with the clock steeple dominates the village square, as does the tower with tiny cars winding around it. The 12″ x 16″ metal pan inside the wicker tray is filled with soil. Black sand is used to denote roads and the square. The mountain in the background is a mound of soil topped with brown sand and a sprinkling of white sand for snow. Green moss and grass make the meadows in the rear, with a "forest" of ivy cuttings (Hedera "Ivalace") and tiny Norfolk Island Pine seedlings (Araucaria excelsa). The "tree" behind one house is a young Syngonium podophyllum, while the other "forest" to the right is made up of several miniature hollies (Malpighia coccigera).

You can always say you're doing this garden to amuse the children on a rainy day, but you love every minute of it! The handmade barn was given to me by a friend, and the animals were purchased at a Christmas fair. After you've filled the inner liner with soil, sow a ground cover of rye grass and "mow" it to a quarter of an inch. Place all the little animals and accessories just where you want them, then add a few small plants for "trees" and "shrubs." Pictured here are Osmanthus fragrans, Podocarpus alpinus, and Jasminum gracile magnificum. Many different plants could be used in such a garden, but one must be taller than the barn to keep everything within some sort of scale.

Here is another easy garden for children to plant, and what a charming scene results from so few plants and so little effort! A round, 8″ basket (lined with plastic) is filled with soil and given a rye-grass cover, cut to about one-quarter inch. It's best if the rye grass is uneven because our farmer's wife is guiding her geese through a meadow not a manicured suburban lawn. I fell in love with this little handmade straw doll at some bazaar, and she gave me this bucolic inspiration. To create a wooded background in the distance, plant a few small-leaved ivy rooted cuttings (with the lower leaves cut off) and any other small-leaved plant. Here I've added young jasmine plants for height and have let some of the rye grass grow tall and droop over the edge for a natural effect.

geese, and ducks are a natural for the courtyard, while pigs and rabbits belong in a fenced-in enclosure.

An all-purpose soil is fine to use for the plants that would be normally found in this type of landscape.

The Woodland Garden.   The simplest and most natural way of doing this landscape is by scooping up a small amount of moss with a few tree seedlings already growing in it. Add a few fine grass seeds and a couple of ferns. Evergreen seedlings can be dug out of the woods (you only need two or three) and so can a bit of moss. Keep them moist in a plastic bag until you get home. A stream or a pond can be made out of fine gravel, sand, or a bit of smoky mirror (regular mirror looks too artificial). Or bury a tiny dark-colored or glass dish in the soil and keep it filled with water. A few deer look perfectly at home in this setting. The size of the container dictates the extent of the landscaping. Adding rock outcroppings is done with pieces of featherock or several flat, smooth stones. If room permits, introduce a ground cover in addition to the moss, such as selaginella kraussiana brownii or Helxine soleirolii (Baby's-tears). Small-leaved ivy with the lower leaves cut off make good trees to go along with the evergreen seedlings. Avoid variegated (green-and-white leaves) or fancy ruffled ivies, since they just don't have the natural look to make it as trees.

A woodland garden is nature at its most natural. Therefore, nothing in your design should look contrived. If you find that a small weed is popping out of the moss you scooped up in the woods, let it be. Trim it to size if it gets out of hand. A few tiny pieces of weathered wood duplicate the rotted logs always found in such woods. The tiniest sinningias are perfect to double as wild flowers. Tuck these among a few ferns. A "path" can be made of very finely shredded peat moss. If you grab a handful of peat moss and rub it between your hands, what's at the bottom of your palm will be extra fine and good to use for paths or under trees. A few seeds of rye

I have to confess that this is one of my favorites. An aluminum-foil baking pan (12" x 16") lines the wicker tray. The starting point is the half-rotted wood log. Behind it is the only plant (other than bulbs) that I've ever left in its pot, a young coffee plant, Coffea arabica. Next to it is the slender and evergraceful Pteris ensiformis "Victoriae." To the extreme left is the dwarf Begonia "Peridot," sending out its flower spikes. Partially hidden in the background, next to the begonia, is an unidentified fern growing and spreading from a piece of moss which I took from my own woods. An entirely different kind of moss, also from my woods, is sending forth tiny white hairy spikes as well as several wild violets. I added Helxine soleiroli so it could dangle over the edge of the wicker. A clump of miniature daffodils adds a bright touch to this woodland garden.

A piece of driftwood and the cover of a 12"
straw basket set the mood for a deep-forest feel-
ing. The tall graceful fern in the back is Pteris
ensiformis "Victoriae," with Nephrolepis exaltata
"Fluffy Ruffles" next to it, and Saxifraga sarmentosa on the surface. To the left, winding its way
through the driftwood, is Asplenium platyneuron
(Ebony Spleenwort) and Selaginella delicatula
spilling over the edge. A ground cover of green
moss completes the design. If you wish, one or
two Sinningia pusilla peeking through the moss
would be an inspired addition. I thought of it too
late to have them show up.

A rocky woodland scene is achieved with a deep
8″ x 10″ container and a large piece of featherock
out of which grows Araucaria excelsa to the left
and Davallia bullata mariesii on the right. Cover
these holes with damp green moss. Lush ferns
grow on the left side, Asplenium cristatum, with
the dwarf Begonia "Granny" at its base. Cover
the rest of the surface with Selaginella kraussiana
(denticulata) and a few clumps of rye grass.

Give a child the few following items and he'll create a charming woodland watering hole for two thirsty deer: one small ivy plant (here Hedera helix "denticulata" which curves to form a shelter), a small piece of damp moss into which has been sown a few seeds of rye grass (to be kept cut unevenly), plus some white or beige gravel for the "dry" stream. And that's it, except of course for the deer, and a plain, dark-colored ceramic dish that's smaller than a dinner plate.

grass, kept pruned, fill out the landscape, giving it a lush look.

A mountain-forest landscape is a variation on the woodland. To give perspective to the scene, the trees must be really tiny at the base of the "mountain," getting smaller the closer they are to the summit, so it will appear to be a mountain, not a hill. One wall of the mountain (made with a mound of soil) can be sheer rock, easily simulated with broken pieces of featherock or flat stones. Give the mountain a snow cap if you desire by sprinkling some white sand over the top very carefully; a tiny bit will do. Fine-bladed grass kept trimmed unevenly is effective at the base of the mountain. Alpine plants are obviously at home in such a setting but are not easy to grow. Soil on the acid side is best with woodland plants.

The Desert Landscape. This is one of the easiest to create and maintain, for nothing more quickly conveys the idea of the desert than a few cacti, a piece of driftwood, and white sand. A large red clay saucer makes a fine container, as does most any kind of simple pottery. Line it with foil, since clay is porous and even though desert gardens should be watered sparingly, not at all in winter, some moisture might seep through and stain the furniture. Have one tall cactus dominating the scenery, with others grouped informally. Add a few succulents, including one of a hanging variety as ground cover. Some jagged pieces of featherock or coral stones simulate the rough terrain of the desert. Pale, smooth, small stones become a "dry valley." What ties it all together is a covering of white sand or perlite on the surface. The old, bent gold prospector with his faithful burro have adorned many such a landscape. For those who want to emphasize the southwestern flavor, by all means add the old boy—if you can find him.

There are so many varieties of cacti and succulents, each one more intriguing than the other, that one would be hard put to find two identical desert landscapes. These plants require as much sun and warmth as you can give them, and a special sandy

A desert scene is so easy to create if you start with a red clay saucer and a piece of featherock with a few holes scooped out of it. Plant Crassula lycopodioides for the interesting spidery effect. Fill the holes with Haworthia subfasciata, Mammillaria bocasana, and Echeveria carnicolor. Sedum allantoides hangs gracefully over the edge. A mulch of perlite ties the whole composition together.

It's easy to see why I call this serene scene "Contemplation." From the moment I saw how beautifully the dwarf Begonia "Folosia" arched its delicate stems to resemble a weeping willow, with a wise Japanese man meditating under its protective cover, I realized that nothing else was needed in this composition, except for a green cover and a tiny lantern for balance. I must honestly add that after more than two years of looking at it, I decided to remove the lantern, and I think it's for the best. Simplicity is the key to this garden. An 18″, shallow, black, unglazed bonsai dish is the only possible container for this design.

Choose a 12″, round bonsai container for your Japanese garden. A temple arch in the background provides distance and a focal point. For "trees," nothing beats a small Dizygotheca elegantissima (left) or the Araucaria excelsa on the right (that's a Norfolk Island Pine seedling). For shrubbery and added greenery, try Crassula argenta and Crassula perforata "Pagoda." The graceful miniature grasses to the left are Acorus gramineus pusillus. A must is a ground cover of Helxine soleiroli (Baby's Tears) or if you prefer, velvety moss. Sprinkle gravel or sand under the tiny bridge. This composition must be viewed at eye level to appreciate its full beauty.

soil. (See page 67, on soil mixtures.) Pruning is not possible in this type of garden. About the only pruning you can do is snipping away at the creeping succulent to keep it within bounds. When plants get overpowering (which takes a few years) remove one or two, or start the garden all over again.

The Japanese Garden. Less is best in this type of garden. The Japanese garden is understated, serene, the essence of simplicity. There are few plants, but they are carefully selected and placed. Empty space is very much a part of the overall design. Space is necessary if a plant is to be high lighted, perspective emphasized, and a generally clean design achieved. How you design the garden depends on your accessories. Limit them to a few: a temple and an archway; a house and bridge over tiny stream; a lantern placed next to a shrub or small stone. Stones themselves have an important meaning in the Japanese garden; how they're placed and what kind of design they make are highly symbolic.

This brings us to the subject of authenticity. To create a genuine Japanese garden, even in miniature, requires knowledge of Japanese cultural and religious traditions. Nothing in such a garden is without meaning and a purpose. If you are a purist and wish to create an authentic Japanese landscape, read one of the many excellent books on the subject first. For our purpose in this book, we are striving for the *suggestion* of a Japanese garden. As with the art of bonsai (see pages 62–66), most people are quite happy with achieving the illusion, getting as much enjoyment from it as purists do from their works of art.

Evergreens are particularly cherished in the Japanese gardens, as are mosses (the moss gardens of Japan are famous), but the cultivation of miniature evergreens requires a very cool room, kept under 60 degrees Fahrenheit. Instead, try the dizygotheca elegantissima (aralia), one of the most Oriental-looking plants. Its delicately cut foliage makes it a superb tree to use with a tiny Jade plant as a shrub. The

Japanses variety of Sweet Flag, Acorus gramineus pusillus, grows to about three inches and has grass-like leaves. Use mosses or Baby's-tears as ground cover. Both require high humidity, so mist them at least once a day.

Miniature Terrariums

Technically, *terrarium* is a term for a covered container without any opening, but it has come to mean any clear glass or plastic dish that has high sides, such as a canister or a brandy snifter. If standard-sized terrariums rely heavily on miniature plants, the tiny version needs them even more. Obviously there can be no attempt at landscaping when dealing with a container as small as a tiny plastic box or a tulip-shaped champagne glass. Yet a charming bit of nature can be cultivated, offering many moments of delightful observation as the plant comes into bloom or simply grows and changes.

Select your diminutive container, and spread on the bottom a layer of the finest gravel you can find. (Pet shops are a good source.) Mix in a few bits of charcoal. Next, pour in slightly moistened sterilized soil (buy a tiny bag of potting soil with perlite already mixed in). Carefully remove the tiny plant from its pot, shake off some of the soil clinging to the roots, and place it inside the terrarium. Add more soil around plant, firming it with your fingers, a chopstick, or a Q-tip. Water most cautiously, enough to wet the soil but not to allow any water to stand at the bottom. Use an eyedropper if terrarium is really tiny, otherwise a clothes sprinkler or a mister will do nicely. To prevent soil from drying out too quickly if terrarium is not airtight, cover the surface with tiny bits of sphagnum moss that have been thoroughly moistened first. This is a good trick to use with any of these littlest of plants, whether in or out of terrariums. It may prevent a disaster if you forget to water for a day or two during hot weather.

A terrarium and a sand painting, all in one covered clear glass container. Sinningias love high humidity, so plant them under cover for best results. The miniature varieties shown are Sinningia pusilla whose lavender flowers go well with those of S. "White Sprite."

Miniature plants that require high humidity, such as the dainty sinnigias, are the best choices for terrariums, but if you wish, you can use seedlings of standard-sized plants. If you do, however, be prepared to cut them back as they start to grow to their normal height, or else take them out and start all over again with another seedling.

All-purpose soil is adequate for terrarium plants. After initial watering, do not water again if container has an airtight cover; just open and check every few months to see if soil is still moist. If you see much condensation building up inside the cover, remove it for one hour, then put back on. But do keep an eye on miniatures in open containers. They should be treated in the same way as all other plants: stick your finger in the soil, then water if the soil feels dry.

Bonsai

Bonsai is the dwarfing of trees by the severe restriction of their roots in small containers. It is a highly developed art, requiring skill, experience, and background knowledge of this ancient Japanese form of gardening. It's practiced by few people in its authentic form in this country, chiefly because the plants must be kept outdoors (on special occasions they're brought indoors to be admired, but only for a day or so). This is so the trees can experience each season outdoors as they normally would were they still growing in their natural state. They must go through dormancy in winter in order to survive. Bonsai, by the way, refers to both container ("bon") and plant ("sai").

There is no reason, however, why one can't have the pleasure of training a bonsai by using ordinary house plants and striving for the same principles of scale, form, and design. The standard bonsai pot is about ten to twelve inches long if it's oblong or five inches across if it's round. Warm-climate plants such as Carissa grandiflora, Malpighia coccigera, old

A geranium bonsai? Why not—if you have or can get an old gnarled plant that already has interesting branching habits. Place the geranium at one side of a small bonsai container, and with thin copper wire you can make it go the way you want it to. This specimen has bloomed off and on for three years, and I never cease to marvel at the graceful sweep of the bottom stem and flower. It works with miniature geraniums, too.

geraniums, rex begonias, small-leaved ivy, "florist" azalea, and podocarpus are popular house plants that lend themselves to bonsai training. Rosemary is a fragrant herb, but its shrublike growth habit also makes it a delight to train in all sorts of interesting shapes. Avoid bushy plants, since they require too much pruning.

All of these plants are fine for regular-sized bonsai pots, but if you want a miniature bonsai, you'll have to use true dwarf varieties of plants. Since bonsai is the miniaturizing of plants to begin with, it appears redundant to speak of creating a "miniature" bonsai, yet it can be done if you start with a tiny container and a dwarf plant. But whichever form you choose, it's a great deal of fun to make your own bonsai, starting with the oddest and oldest plant you can find. Look for a plant that has gnarled stems or unusual branching. Leggy or odd-looking geraniums that you would normally reject at the plant shop are precisely right for bonsai training.

Potting a bonsai is simplicity itself. Cover the bottom of the container with wire mesh or a layer of finely broken shard to prevent the soil from spilling out the drainage holes. If using the mesh, add a layer of small pebbles on top. Add appropriate soil (this means soil suited to the plants' needs, which in most cases is the ordinary potting mixture described on page 67).

Do not place the plant in the center of the container. Asymmetry is the key. Your bonsai can be trained in either the "triangle" or the "upright" style. In the latter, the plant is allowed to develop in an informal manner, the curve of the trunk and the branches growing in an interesting free form. There is no "front" or "back" to the plant. For the triangle style, select the side of the plant that lends itself most to obtaining unusual branch formation. Have a finished design in mind, selecting three branches of uneven lengths that will be used to form a triangle. Having chosen the three branches (they're really stems, since we're working with house plants), cut off any others. Start pruning the remaining three branches very slowly and carefully. Cut off one leaf at a time until you have the desired effect. Snip away at the branches with equal care. Step back after each cut to see how the entire plant looks from a few feet away. If you have chosen a plant with an interesting shape, you probably have branches that are already heading in the direction you want, so you'll have little if any wiring to do.

If you wish a branch to be lowered, raised, or curved more than it already is, wiring is the solution. Using thin copper wire, sink one end of it at least one inch into the soil to anchor it; then wrap it around the trunk and the branches you wish to remold, bending the wire into the position you want. Wrap it tightly enough around the branch so that the latter will eventually grow in the new direction. Leave the wire on for several months; then remove it carefully. Don't wait until the wire cuts into the branch. When you see this happen, remove wire immediately.

Cut off the new shoots that appear, since the objective is to keep within the dimensions of the design you have created as well as to reveal the lines of the trunk. A clearly visible trunk from bottom to top of plant is an important element of bonsai. Depending on the plant, the trunk may not be very high, but whatever there is of it should be readily seen. On flowering plants, such as a geranium, cut off faded flowers quickly to insure the growth of new ones. A covering of green moss on the surface of the soil gives a finished look. Keep it moist to preserve its velvety green texture. Small polished black stones, usually found in Oriental shops, can also be used to cover the soil. These mulches are not only attractive but help to keep the roots and the soil moist.

The smallest, simplest bonsai pot is best for miniatures, especially if you are working with dwarf plants. Make sure it has a drainage hole and a matching saucer. If gnarled roots appear on the surface, let them be. This is all part of bonsai culture. But roots coming out of the drainage hole should be cut off.

Keep the plant out of direct sunlight and drafts, and water frequently, since the roots eventually take up most of the pot and little soil is left. Roots should never be allowed to dry out.

Soil Mixtures

So little soil is needed for miniature gardens that soil weight is not a factor. It is therefore unnecessary to resort to soilless mixes, with their special fertilizing requirements. Good soil is vital to the health of plants. They draw nourishment and moisture from it. Miniature plants require the same type of soil as do standard plants. A dwarf begonia is happy in the soil appropriate for a regular begonia; a miniature geranium will thrive in the same mixture blended for its large-sized relatives. What is important is that the mixture be suitable for the kind of plant, that it hold moisture, and that it drain well.

There are three basic types of soil mixtures: a "normal" or average mixture appropriate for the majority of house plants, an "acid" mixture for such plants as begonias and ferns, and another mixture for cacti and succulents. It's easy to see why plants with different soil requirements can't be grown in the same container.

Always start with fresh, sterilized soil. This is readily available in small plastic bags in plant shops and variety stores. Even if all you need are three tablespoons of soil, don't go out and scoop it up outside. Why risk having the bugs or diseases already in that soil? It's bad enough that you may have to cope with such pests later on, so at least you should start with pure ingredients.

Packaged soil is usually too "heavy," meaning too rich, to be used as it comes out of the bag. It needs to be diluted with sand or perlite. The latter is by far easier and lighter to work with. Peat moss is also added to the mixture so that it will retain moisture and have the proper acid properties. If a potting mixture calls for leaf mold (or humus, which is the same thing) and you can't get it, simply increase the percentage of peat moss. Peat moss is less acid than leaf mold or humus and may be used in larger quantities.

Bone meal is an excellent addition to potting mixtures because it's a slow-acting fertilizer, high in nitrogen and phosphoric acid. Also, it can be used safely, without fear of burning the roots.

Potting Mixture No. 1 (for most house plants)
2 parts loam (packaged soil)
1 part peat moss
1 part sand or perlite
1 teaspoon bone meal per quart of mixture
1 teaspoon limestone per quart of mixture (optional)
Mix all ingredients *thoroughly.*

Potting Mixture No. 2 (for acid-loving plants)
1 part loam
1 part peat moss
1 part sand or perlite
1 teaspoon bone meal per quart of mixture
Mix all ingredients *thoroughly.*

Potting Mixture No. 3 (for most cacti, succulents)
1 part loam
1 part sand or perlite
½ part very small bits of broken clay pots, broken bricks, or Turface (a coarse processed clay)
1 teaspoon bone meal per quart of mixture
1 teaspoon limestone per quart of mixture
Mix all ingredients *thoroughly.*

It's safe to state that these three potting mixtures should take care of practically all the soil needs of the miniature-plant gardener, with the exception of exotics such as orchids or bromeliads. Out-of-the-ordinary plants are usually purchased from specialists, who in turn furnish you with the necessary culture information to keep the plants healthy.

Some packaged potting soil now comes with perlite included, although not enough. If you see lots of white specs in the soil, fluffy white granules, this is perlite; simply cut down on the amount of perlite specified in the potting mixture. It's important that the ingredients be thoroughly mixed. You can do this easily on newspapers over the kitchen counter or inside a plastic bag. Keep whatever is left over in a double plastic bag tightly closed with a twist-tie.

3.

Gardens in
Sand

When a bouquet has faded, what to do with the florist's goblet that held it? If it's opaque white glass, plant it, but if it's clear glass, try a sand painting before planting it. Start with a bottom layer of perlite, plus one of brightly colored gravel, for good drainage; then alternate layers of colored sand. Use a potting mixture for the top layer. Stemmed containers are ideal for at least one trailing plant, such as the burro's tail, Sedum morganianum, shown here with a peanut cactus about to bloom, Chamaecereus silvestri. (Pluck off the "peanuts" as plant gets too big and use them elsewhere.) Add a tall cactus in the background, and you have a striking miniature garden. Sprinkle a layer of white sand or perlite on top to give it a finished look.

Sand "painting," whether of abstract or scenic designs, became a popular hobby a few years ago. Booklets are readily available giving detailed instructions on how to go about doing a seascape, a lion's head, or a chain of snow-capped mountains, to name a few. These sand designs are the primary attraction, with plants taking a secondary place. The gardener, however, is chiefly interested in plants. A compromise is to use a low-key abstract design in sand, which will not compete with the plants for attention. My personal opinion is that abstract designs are more imaginative than realistic landscapes, anyway, and if you make a mistake while sand painting, no one will be wiser; it just becomes part of the design.

First, select a container. It can be anything made of clear glass or plastic. It should be sufficiently deep to allow for at least two to three inches of sand plus another inch, at the very least, of soil. Plastic cubes, giant champagne glasses, extra-large cocktail glasses, and tall glass kitchen canisters that stack are all good containers. Two or three of the latter, each on top of the other, become smashing terrariums requiring humidity-loving plants.

Clear plastic flowerpots are also good, and don't forget small wine decanters. Let your imagination go. Look at your glassware and kitchen accessories with a new eye. Picture plants growing out of them with layers of colorful sand as their base. The taller the container, the more layers you can have. Room for less than three layers is inadequate. The fun of sand painting is in the vivid results achieved by combining several colors of sand, each layer deep enough to be plainly seen.

The only tools you need are a knitting needle and a spoon. The first is used to poke into the sand to create a design. The space made by the needle is automatically filled by the sand on the layer above it. For example, if you have a layer of blue sand below a layer of white, poke through the white into the blue, and white sand will flow into the blue. The design you create depends on how you jiggle the needle. After you've done it a few times, you'll quickly catch on. A delicate touch and a certain amount of daring are needed in trying out wild color combinations. Sand painting is one art form in which the only way to learn is by doing. Explicit, well-illustrated directions are indispensable for intricate designs, but there's nothing like actually getting the feel of it. Be prepared to mess up your first few designs, but don't throw away the sand. Mix them up and use the new color as a foundation for another painting or as center filling. No one sees what's inside the core of the container.

The spoon is used to pour the sand. For large amounts, pour the sand out of its bag against the back of the spoon. For small amounts, use the spoon in its normal manner. For instance, here's how to paint a bird:

Pour a layer of blue sand (the sky) into the container. With the spoon, pour a tiny mound of white sand on top of the blue, right against the side of the container, touching the glass. Now stick the knitting needle through the center of the white mound. Withdraw needle carefully. With the spoon, add blue sand on top of and all around the white, and you'll see a white bird flying against a blue sky. Try it a few times so that you get the proportions right. A huge bird in a small container will be out of scale. Realists use a deeper shade of blue for the ocean, brown for mountains, white for snow on top of the mountains, green for grass, and so forth. If you prefer the abstract, select the colors with care, then alternate layers, twirling the container after each one and using the needle to create patterns. No two will be alike. Therein lies its appeal.

As mentioned earlier, you can use anything to fill in the center of the container, but this applies only if the container is wide. If not, it will be too difficult to pour the colored sand against the glass and something else in the middle. It will all blend, and the money you thought you saved will go toward buying more sand and starting all over again. It's safer, with narrow containers, to stick with the desired color of sand.

Procedures vary with the size and shape of the container, but as a rule of thumb, stop the sand painting about two thirds of the way up the container. Add a layer of black sand or tiny black gravel, and then sprinkle bits of charcoal on top. Let it stand for a few minutes to settle. Now add the potting soil, pressing it down gently. Take the plants out of their pots, and slowly and carefully place them in the container, adding more soil as needed. Firm soil around each plant with your fingers or the spoon. Water sparingly (not at all if plants are cacti or succulents; wait a few weeks before watering them). Water should go down through the soil but not into the sand painting —not that it would do the garden any harm, but tiny bits of soil might find their way through. For a finished look, top off with a layer of perlite, white sand, or small white gravel if the plants are cacti or succulents. For others, use green moss (thoroughly moistened before putting down) or another layer of the same black pebbles. Besides being attractive, a mulch keeps the roots cool and reduces dehydration of the soil.

As to selection of plants, much depends on the depth of the soil. Most cacti and succulents are shallow rooted, so that they would be good choices. Besides, they somehow seem to go best with sand paintings. However, any dwarf plant will do. Sinningias are perfect for the stacked, covered canisters. Also try African violets, begonias, ferns, or dwarf geraniums. If you have room for more than one plant, create interest by having one taller than the other, perhaps an upright cactus with a trailing succulent.

Colored sand is available at a variety of gift stores as well as some plant shops. Save mayonnaise, pickle, or jelly jars because they make great storage containers for the sand. By placing the jars next to one another, you'll spot easily which color combinations you like. Expect to use more of the black and white than the colored sand, since they are good color separators.

4 ✼

Gardens in Water

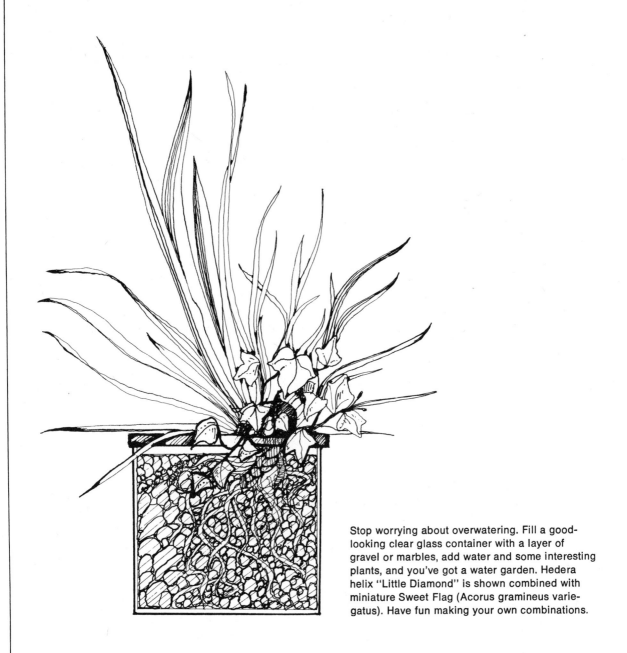

Stop worrying about overwatering. Fill a good-looking clear glass container with a layer of gravel or marbles, add water and some interesting plants, and you've got a water garden. Hedera helix "Little Diamond" is shown combined with miniature Sweet Flag (Acorus gramineus variegatus). Have fun making your own combinations.

If proper watering of standard-sized plants is a problem for indoor gardeners, watering miniature gardens is an even greater challenge. It's easy to water too little or too much. (See Chapter 8.) If the task proves too much for you or you've already lost several plants or you travel a good deal and have no one to "plant-sit," then growing plants in water is for you. There is no second guessing on how much water the plant needs.

Many house plants can be grown as successfully in water as in soil. Even a landscape can be created, and you can group several containers to make an attractive design.

Select your mini-container. It can be clear or opaque. If it's clear glass or plastic, expect algae to form more rapidly because of the sunlight. Don't have too shallow a container or you'll be constantly refilling it with water; the main advantage of this type of gardening is freedom with regard to watering schedules. Stay away from metal pots (copper, lead, brass) because of possible harmful chemical reactions. The container must be absolutely clean; wash it in soap and water with household bleach added. If your municipal water system has chlorine in it, fill a pitcher with water and let it stand for a couple of days. This will remove the chlorine. A water softener is also injurious to plants.

Practically all foliage house plants can be grown in water, although some, such as aglaonema, coleus, dracaena, dieffenbachia, ivies, fatshedera, philodendrons, Scindapsus, tradescantia, zebrina, and plectranthus, do better than others (see Chapter 9 for a listing of plants). Choose small plants. When you've made your selection, knock the plant gently out of its pot, place it in a bowl, and submerge the roots in water for ten minutes to loosen the soil. Holding the plant gingerly by its stem, wash the rest of the soil off the roots under the tap, but make sure the flow of water is a mere trickle. You don't want to injure any of the delicate roots. When the plant is thoroughly clean of all soil, it's ready for planting in water.

As with miniature gardens in soil, it's important

to keep scale in mind. It won't do to have a wine glass holding large-leaved philodendron, even if you anchor the roots properly. It will look top-heavy. Stick with small-leaved plants.

You will need material to anchor the plants inside the container. Builder's sand, pearl chips, or the small gravel used for terrariums or aquariums are good. Avoid vivid or multicolored gravel, since they compete with the plants. Rinse the material well before using it. Spread a few inches of the material inside the container, mixing some small charcoal bits with it to keep the water sweet smelling. Position the plants where you want them on top of the material, adding more around the plants to anchor them securely. Add water to about one half to three quarters the depth of the material. Remove leaves lying below the surface of the anchoring material.

Every time you add water—and this includes the initial watering—add a weak liquid fertilizer at the rate of one quarter the recommended dosage listed by the manufacturer. Check once a week, more often during hot summer months, to make sure water remains at the same level. While this may appear to be a nuisance, remember that all you have to do is add fertilized water. Gone is the worry of *how much* water to give the plants. You just pour to the desired level, and that's it for another week. No agony over underwatering or overwatering.

Plants can also be grown directly in water without benefit of an anchoring material if the container is deep, such as a pitcher. This is an excellent way of rooting cuttings given to you by friends and enjoying an attractive display at the same time. When the cuttings have developed roots, you can then plant them in shallower containers with gravel, as previously described. You also need to add bits of charcoal and a weak fertilizer to the water. Every few months, empty the whole thing, wash pot and roots, and refill. The smaller the pot, the more quickly the water evaporates, so keep an eye on it.

If you have a garden (or a friend with one), cut a few small branches of forsythia, pussy willow, or weeping willow in early spring, and watch the buds open slowly as roots develop in water. Pull out one or two pachysandra or myrtle plants while you're at it, since these do well in water too.

5

Dollhouse
Gardens

The fervor of collectors of miniature furniture and accessories for dollhouses can only be understood after attending one of their regional exhibits. Children go from booth to booth clutching their few dollar bills, to be spent only after agonizing decisions, while adults head for the rare and the antique. Besides furniture, every conceivable accessory is available: kitchen utensils, fireplace equipment, rugs, curtains, mirrors, comforters, paintings, chandeliers, lamps; miniature foods and candies to be set on miniature tables complete with tiny candles and tea sets. How about a miniature copy of *The New York Times* with the breakfast tray? It's for sale. Added to all these are planters and pots filled with plastic flowers as well as artificial shrubbery for outside the house. Why not the real thing?

Obviously, the Lilliputian size of dollhouse pots sharply limits what can be planted in them. Only the most minute seedlings with the smallest of root balls can make it, and be prepared to replace them periodically. The investment is practically zero, however, so I'm not recommending extravagance. I have found that tiny cacti and succulents are best, since they have such small roots and need very little moisture. Considering how quickly these smaller-than-a-thimble pots dry out, *this is a vital factor.* The so-called peanut cactus is a good plant source, since each segment of the plant, or "peanut," is easily snapped off and rooted in the sand filling the doll pot. Small-leaved, creeping succulents are also in good proportion to such pots.

When planting your midget container, make sure the soil is very fine. Crumble it between your fingers until it's powdery. Use a sandy mixture for cacti and succulents, a regular one for other plants. Dampen the soil with a few drops of water. With a toothpick, make a hole and insert the plant, using the toothpick to firm the soil around the plant. Use an eyedropper for watering. Give the plants some extra light by taking them out of the dollhouse daily for a couple of hours.

Landscaping can be done outside the dollhouse

I bought the dollhouse miniatures at one of the regional miniatures shows and planted the tiny basket on the floor and the clay pot on the table stand with Sedum dasyphyllum. The metal container on the table and the clay pot on the floor hold little peanut cacti, Chamaecereus silvestri. The "log basket" is filled with a few twigs. Two years later, everything is still growing (yet both clay pots are less than half an inch high).

as well. Window boxes look charming filled with seedlings (when seeds sprout and the second pair of leaves appear, you have just about the tiniest plant at your disposal, no matter what the variety). If the window boxes are deep enough (all depends on the size of the dollhouse; some are very large), plant dwarf geraniums. Use dwarf evergreens, euonymus, and ivy as "foundation" plants around the house. Plant them in tiny containers, and group them at the base of the house and on either side of the entrance. Plants must be in scale to the house to be most effective. Create a terrace behind the house with tubbed plants and outdoor furniture (readily available in wood or metal, in all sorts of styles and sizes). How much "landscaping" you do around the house depends on how it's displayed and how much room you have to work with. Use your imagination.

This type of miniature gardening is fun and should not be taken too seriously. But it's a challenge to any gardener if ever there was one. Here are some examples: a miniature early-American washtub is two and three eighths inches in diameter and one and one quarter inches deep. It's wooden, with brass handles. It can double as a planter for indoors or out. Add a bird bath surrounded by potted plants. A garden tool set can be purchased (one and five eighths inches long), to be casually placed to one side of the terrace.

6.

Miniature Rock Gardens

As with designing a rock garden outdoors, it's the placement of the rocks that is most important to achieving a natural-looking landscape. The "rocks" can be made of pieces of featherock (a natural stone made of lava foam from the volcanoes of the Sierra Nevada mountains of northern California) available at most garden centers, or use any stones of rugged appearance. A trip to the beach will yield some fine specimens. Stick to one color for a unifying effect. Wash the rocks thoroughly to remove any traces of salt. Search for unusually shaped stones along country roads or in your own back yard (or that of a friend). The more natural the stones look, the better. You may make an exception to this if you wish to display a large semiprecious stone such as a rose quartz which then becomes a focal point with plants as backdrop.

Select a simple, shallow container, filling it halfway to the top with soil, after first having spread a layer of small gravel or broken shard for drainage. Arrange the stones in an informal design, leaning on one another as casually as possible. Sprinkle soil between the stones for planting. Gently knock the plants out of their pots and do a "dry run" of where you want to place them. Keep changing them around until your eye tells you that you've got the most pleasing and natural-looking design.

The tiniest of dwarf plants are used to fill in the cracks in the stones: sedum with minute leaves and trailing stems, dwarf Baby's-tears, Corsican mint (Mentha requiena). The base of the stones is a good spot for a clump of miniature grasses (Acorus gramineus pusillus). Plant varieties that most closely resemble wild flowers are best for rock gardens, as opposed to such flowering plants as African violets, roses, and geraniums. Miniature alpine plants are superb but not easy to obtain or cultivate. There are so many kinds of cacti and succulents in all shapes and sizes that these plants are the easiest for the beginner to work with. All plants selected should have the same culture requirements. Mixing plants

Any simple clay container makes a proper setting for a tiny rock garden. Take your time placing the stones so they look natural. Cracks are filled with Echeveria derenbergii, Crassula Schmidtii, and Haworthia radula, with Sedum dasyphyllum as ground cover. For balance, choose your favorite column-shaped cactus.

that need lots of moisture with those that like it dry leads to disaster.

If you have a large piece of featherock, it's easy to hollow out a "crevice" or a few pockets with a hammer and chisel. Drill holes all the way to the bottom for proper drainage, although I confess that I didn't do it on mine and have not lost a plant because of it. Featherock is so porous that water quickly dissipates, but if possible, play it safe and drill the holes. When everything is planted, water very gently, so as not to disturb the plants and soil. A good way of doing this is to trickle the water down the rocks until it moistens the plants in and around it. Use a small paper cup with the lip pinched to form a slow trickle.

7.

How to Display Miniature Gardens in the Home

Growing plants is one thing, displaying them is another. Scattering pots around the house, no matter what their size, is ineffective, diluting their potential in contributing a great deal of beauty to the interior decoration of the home. When plants and containers are very tiny, the challenge increases. A thimble on a coffee table risks being constantly knocked over, but there are ways of showing off miniature gardens to best advantage. After all the time and care you took to put them together, you want to be able to admire them, follow their daily growth, and groom them with ease. Let's explore a few ideas on placement of miniature gardens.

Window sills and glass shelves across the window are best bets for desert scenes with cacti and succulents, since these require a great deal of sun. This is also true of flowering plants such as geraniums. Place sand gardens a bit higher than eye level on a shelf, to let the viewer see the various layers of colors. Containers with stems (such as a giant champagne glass) are also better shown a bit above eye level, since they will usually hold a hanging plant. Shells, thimbles, egg cups, and all tiny pots are most effective at eye level, while landscaped dish gardens are best viewed slightly below eye level. An exception to this is when perspective plays a role, as in a garden scene that is planted with taller "trees" in the foreground, leading the eye to a garden gate or smaller "trees" in the distance. This must be at eye level to be fully appreciated.

Moving away from the window, miniature gardens of shade-loving plants such as begonias, peperomias, or ferns and mosses, which would be found in a woodland scene, are effective on a tabletop, as long as the latter is not too cluttered with other items. Even if the garden is a large one by miniature standards, it shouldn't have to compete with stacks of books, ashtrays, and yesterday's mail for attention. Strive for simplicity in the overall design. A garden under a lamp is ideal, since it will be highlighted at night. Also, in the winter when the days are short, the plants will get extra light from the lamp. The tiny

A jewel of a glass vitrine, brass-trimmed and only four and a half inches high, holds your precious and certainly your tiniest plants. From top to bottom: straw basket is filled with Sedum dasyphyllum and Echeveria derenbergii sending forth its lovely rosette; a glass-duck salt cellar has Sedum cuspidatum; a dollhouse-size straw basket obviously is large enough for a tiny amount of Sedum dasyphyllum because it's been there over a year and still thriving; the engraved brass cup is filled with Echeveria subsessilis (E. peacockii) while the thimble holds one "peanut cactus," Chamaecereus; teacup with a bird as handle is easily filled with any tiny cactus found at local dime stores.

size of the container is insurance that the heat from the bulb will not injure the plants, since they will be far enough away from the lamp. A rock garden or a landscape scene should be displayed alone. Don't crowd it with other plants, especially those of standard size.

What about the tiniest of containers, such as teacups, thimbles, wine glasses, and salt cellars? These are best grouped together, three or more are sufficient to make a "statement." Fish bowls or oversized brandy snifters normally used for cut flowers make great display cases for small plants that like humidity. Fill one quarter of the snifter with vermiculite. This is most beneficial for plants, such as sinningias, that like high humidity because it nearly duplicates the atmosphere of a terrarium. If you have a fish tank, clean it thoroughly with a final rinse of water and household bleach. Add a layer of pebbles, then another of vermiculite. Depending on the size of the tank, you can easily display your entire collection of tiny plants in this manner, but only if they all share the same need for high humidity. Don't crowd plants inside a large container, since this makes for very poor air circulation and it doesn't show off each plant to its fullest. As the eye moves from one plant to the next, it must have an instant of repose in between to appreciate fully the singular beauty of each.

A good-looking waterproof tray or a shallow platter also displays tiny containers well, as long as the trays are not covered with floral or bold designs. This detracts from the plants and their containers. Stick with solid-color trays and platters. Increase humidity for the plants by adding a layer of pebbles on the platter (gravel bought at pet shops is good). By keeping the pebbles moist all the time, the plants soak up the humidity as it rises. Pebbles also unify the design, tying all the little plants together, much the same way that mulch does for foundation plants or flowerbeds outdoors.

Grouping plants for maximum effect follows the same principles as arranging bric-a-brac. A knowledgeable eye is the final arbiter. Use your imagina-

If you're really into tiny, tiny pots, group them all on a dinner plate, preferably a heavy pottery one in a solid color. The elaborately decorated porcelain Easter egg on the left is planted with Sedum bellum and Crassula orbicularis with perlite on the surface (white sand would do as well). The two vividly colored miniature Chinese vases in the foreground have a tiny cactus in one and Sedum dasyphyllum trailing from the other. In the back, from left to right: a small Oriental brass bowl with Mammillaria prolifera (pusilla), a clam shell with two Graptopetalum paraguayense (Sedum Weinbergii) growing like twin towers, while the tiniest teacup, almost dollhouse size, holds a Kalanchoe tubiflora seedling.

tion, and move plants around until you have a pleasing design. You will know instinctively that a miniature landscape of important proportions will look fabulous all alone on its own table or shelf. This is especially true of bonsai. There is something to the spartan simplicity of the design of plant and container that demands contemplation in solitude. A bonsai is in the category of specimen plants, or "standards," which should be shown alone. Check to see which is the "good" side of the bonsai, and place it accordingly.

A miniature terrarium shouldn't be in direct sunlight. Include it with your other little plants on a tray. If you have more than one terrarium, group them together on a shallow platter. Diminutive hanging baskets are placed according to their light needs. Hang a trailing sedum in a south window or whichever one gets the most sun in your home. It will look prettiest if it hangs above your other tiny gardens as part of a unit. Hang a fern or any other shade-loving plant in a north window or a spot several feet away from a window. Three or more little baskets hanging together at different levels are an attractive sight.

Artificial lighting is beneficial to plants, no matter what their size, and also provides a dramatic way of showing them off. You can buy small, ready-made units that are handsome enough to put in your living room, on an end table or a low chest; or add fluorescent tubes over one or two bookshelves. Tubes come in many lengths and sizes, so you are bound to find some to fit your space. Two tubes side by side are required as well as a white reflector to focus the light directly on the plants. Figure on twenty watts of light for every square foot of plants, kept on from twelve to sixteen hours a day, depending on whether they're foliage or flowering plants. Place the tubes anywhere from six to twelve inches from the edge of the pot. Plants will shortly let you know the correct distance if you watch for certain signs. If they become leggy, they need additional light, which means place them closer to the tube. If the leaves curl under as if shrinking away from too much light, that's precisely what's going on; place them farther away from the tube. Light is most powerful under the center of the tube, so place your plants according to their needs, the more shade-loving ones near the edges, the sun-craving ones in the center.

You can hide the tube and reflector on bookshelves by adding a strip of molding wide enough to cover the unit below the shelf. The indoor plant boom has brought about an enormous increase in good-looking ready-made units, for tabletops, to hang on the wall or from the ceiling, or to stand on the floor. Scout around your city or send for information from mail order houses specializing in this field (see list on pages 131–35). While house plants may do well with good natural light, there is no denying that they flourish under artificial light. It could make the difference between plants holding their own and growing to their maximum, producing blooms in the case of flowering plants. Cacti and succulents need strong light to flower, and when they do, it's a spectacular sight. Consider artificial lighting if you go in for flowering plants. You'll be richly rewarded.

8.

Care of the Miniature Garden

Watering

This is the most crucial factor in caring for dish gardens. The less soil in a container, the more quickly it dries out. Growing plants in thimbles is a novel idea, but be prepared to water them at least once a day, and sometimes more frequently, depending on the time of year and location. This is the reason why I recommend sticking with succulents and cacti when it comes to planting in the tiniest containers.

Fortunately, indoor gardens are usually located in areas throughout the house that make them difficult to be overlooked. After all, why bother to design and plant a miniature garden if no one can see it? Get into the habit of checking the dryness of the soil surface every time you pass the container. Have a midget watering can handy, or better still, make your own with a small paper cup, folding its lip so that you get only a trickle of water passing through. For really minuscule pots, use an eyedropper.

If the container has no drainage holes, extra care must be taken to make sure that you're not over-watering the plant. This is very easy to do in a tiny pot. Again, cacti and succulents are best for these tiny, drainless containers because they require very little water and can go for weeks without any moisture. When you do water them, give them just a few drops. Other plants are more demanding. You have to water the root ball thoroughly without letting any water collect at the bottom of the pot—a tricky job. To deny it would be less than honest, for the business of watering dish gardens is their only drawback.

However, loss of plants can be greatly reduced by being forewarned. Be on the alert to water *frequently but sparingly.* This is the opposite of what should be done with standard-sized plants in pots with drainage holes, which must be thoroughly soaked and then allowed to go dry before the next watering. Obviously, the trusted finger test can't always be done when the pot is hardly wide enough to hold a fingernail, but you should, whenever possible, stick your finger in the soil and feel if it's damp. If it is, leave the plant alone; if the soil feels dry, water. Try the toothpick method for really tiny pots. The soil is still moist enough if the toothpick leaves a hole or some soil clings to it. If it's sandy and rolls right off the toothpick, the soil is dry and needs watering.

Don't despair if your hand was a bit too quick and you poured more water than you intended into the pot and the plant is swimming. Take it out of the pot, pour out the excess water, and add some fresh dry soil. Don't water again until it needs it. And promise to be more careful in the future.

With pots that have drainage holes, there's no problem. Simply water thoroughly until the water comes out the hole, then let the soil dry out before watering again.

Viterra Hydrogel, a water-retaining product relatively new on the market, can be mixed with your potting soil to prevent it from drying out too quickly. The granules absorb and hold over twenty times their weight in water, which helps to reduce the number of waterings you have to make. It comes in small packages, complete with instructions. If you are unable to buy it locally, W. Atlee Burpee Co. carries it in their catalog (see page 131).

Pruning

Plants can require pruning for two reasons: if part of the plant is dead, diseased, or damaged; or if the plant has grown too large or in an unattractive direction. All dead leaves and stems should be removed. Always cut back well into the healthy growth so you can be certain that the diseased portion has been thoroughly cut out. Faded blossoms should also be removed. If you have selected true miniature varieties, you shouldn't have too much pruning to do to keep them shapely and within the size you desire. However, if you used seedlings or tiny plants of standard varieties, you'll have some pruning to do as the plant grows, for even though its roots will be restricted in a small container, it nevertheless will try its best to keep on growing as nature intended. Cut the plant back periodically with a pair of manicuring scissors. It's better to prune a little bit frequently than to wait until you have to cut off quite a lot. This prevents the possibility of shock and makes for a more attractive plant.

In a landscape scene, pruning is needed to keep the "trees" from growing lower leaves (snip these off as they appear) and "shrubs" from becoming overpowering. Use the same tiny scissors to "mow" the grass and keep the scenery neat. Be careful, however, when it comes to woodland scenes. Their unkempt appearance, totally natural, is their charm, and nothing should look manicured there. Allow some weeds to make an appearance, as long as they're not big ones, and let a clump of grass grow here and there as it wishes.

Transplanting

There's no need to be afraid of transplanting a plant from one container to another. Beginners are sometimes apprehensive about moving plants, yet they shouldn't be if a few precautions are taken. The need to transplant is usually because a plant has outgrown its pot, or you may at last have found the perfect plant for a particular landscape garden and you wish to put it in the place of another plant, which you in turn transplant somewhere else. If you have used seedlings of standard-sized plants, you will be faced with transplanting sooner or later in order to keep everything in scale in a tiny container.

Never transplant in brilliant sunlight. This dries out tiny roots quickly. With a teaspoon, scoop out the plant from its dish without disturbing those around it. If the plant's roots are entangled with those of other plants, gently pull them away until they separate. Some roots will be cut or damaged in this case; compensate for this by snipping off a bit of the top growth (except for palms and ferns). Make sure you get as much of the root ball out as possible. If you're putting the plant by itself in a pot, have the latter ready, with drainage material (bits of broken shard or pebbles) at the bottom and soil halfway up the pot. Put the plant in and add more soil, firming it down with your fingers. Water thoroughly until water comes out drainage hole. If you're putting the plant among others in another dish garden, have the hole ready before digging out the plant. Transfer it quickly, firming soil around the stem, and water just a tiny bit if it's a drainless container. If the plant to be transplanted is already in a pot, knock the side of the pot gently until the plant comes out. Shake off excess soil before planting it in its new home. As a final touch, prune back the plant slightly by pinching its tip to compensate for any loss of roots. Don't put the plant any deeper or higher in the soil than it was before.

If you follow these few simple suggestions, there should be no loss of plant material from transplanting. Speed is important, which is the reason you should have everything ready before you dig up the plant. Don't fertilize it for a month or so; it needs to settle down, not to get a sudden booster shot. When transplanting cacti, use gloves or a tweezer to hold the prickly plant.

Disease and Pest Control

Miniature plants are as prone to ailments as are their larger cousins. As with all plants, prevention of pests and diseases is far easier than control later on. To start off, buy only healthy plants from a reputable plant shop or a mail order firm. Use the correct soil (see page 67) for the plant and water with care (see pages 99–100). Don't crowd the plants too much, although I know that's difficult in a landscape scene in which a lush effect is desired. Good air circulation is necesary to prevent fungus diseases.

Groom plants on a steady weekly basis. This

means picking off any dead leaves or broken foliage. If they're allowed to stay on the surface of the soil, they'll rot, inviting diseases and pests. It's hard to wash leaves of miniature plants, but ivy especially should be rinsed periodically to prevent spider mites. One way to do this is to use a Q-tip dipped in water to clean the leaves. Fortunately, not many leaves are involved in these little gardens, so it's not a chore.

As you are grooming your plants, look them over carefully for signs of pests. Many insects can be spotted by the naked eye, but a magnifying glass is a big help. The most likely insects to be found on house plants are spider mites, aphids, mealybugs, and scales. Some leave a sticky substance on the leaves, which ends up looking like black soot. Pick off any insects you see, or wipe them off with a Q-tip dipped in warm, soapy water. If your infested plant is by itself in a pot, cover the soil with aluminum foil, and, turning the plant upside down, dip it into a soapy solution. Swish it around a few times, then let it dry naturally. Later, rinse the plant the same way and isolate it from others for a few days. If insects return, you may have to resort to a house plant insecticide spray. Make sure it's for *indoor* use, and follow the manufacturer's directions very carefully. There are multipurpose sprays available that kill more than one kind of insect and control fungus disease as well. Never spray near food areas or around people and pets. Here are some of the more common pests and how to control them:

Aphids: Usually found around new growth and buds. They come in many colors and varieties. They're sucking insects with soft bodies, sometimes called plant lice. For control, use a Q-tip dipped in alcohol or a house plant spray that contains malathion.

Cyclamen Mites: These are tricky because you can't see them. Look for deformed buds, wrinkled curled leaves. They prefer the young parts of the plant. They are highly contagious to other plants, so isolate quickly. Control with special miticide spray made for mites.

Mealybugs: These are commonly spotted because they look like little balls of cotton. They are actually soft-bodied sucking insects. Remove them with a Q-tip dipped in rubbing alcohol or nail polish remover, or use a spray containing malathion.

Red Spider Mites: These mites are also invisible to the naked eye. Eventually you'll spot fine cobwebs in between leaves and stems. In the final stages, leaves look like transparent lace. Don't wait until then to control them with a special miticide made just for mites.

Scales: Unfortunately, there are lots of varieties of these sucking insects, mostly gray or brown, with either soft or hard shells. A spray containing malathion controls them.

Whiteflies: These are real pests and hard to control once they've started their prolific reproductive cycles. They're easily spotted by their tiny white wings, which form a cloud when you shake the plant. They suck juices from the leaves, excreting a sticky substance on them which turns into sooty mold. A spray containing synthetic pyrethrum does the best job of controlling them. Repeat the treatment two or three times a few days apart, on the undersides of leaves. This way, you kill several cycles and keep the pests under control.

The typical home is not humid enough to encourage fungus, bacterial and virus diseases in plants, but when these do occur, the only treatment is to discard the plant. It's very hard to distinguish one disease from the other and know precisely which chemical to use. If picking off the affected leaves and applying a fungicide such as benomyl or a Bordeaux mixture doesn't do the trick, it's best to discard the plant. Root rot, stem rot, crown rot to name but a few diseases, are tough to control once the plant has been affected.

Note that ferns are very sensitive to malathion, so if you spray a dish garden with a solution containing this chemical, cover the ferns with a plastic bag. If ferns themselves need spraying, use nicotine sulfate and soap.

Also note that the word *control* has been used repeatedly, not *eradication.* Insects multiply at such a rapid pace that you're doing fine if all you have left are a couple of them. Of course, tiny plants are more quickly damaged and more sensitive than their larger counterparts, but even so, don't strive for perfection in getting rid of your insects. Constant spraying is not good for plants, you, your family, or the environment, so use restraint.

Fertilizing

It might seem that dwarf plants shouldn't be fertilized, for, after all, the main purpose is to keep them small. Stimulating their growth would defeat the purpose. However, we mustn't lose sight of the fact that these mini-plants have the same culture needs as their standard-sized relatives insofar as light, air, and soil are concerned. All living plants can use a boost from time to time, especially those growing in a tiny amount of soil, which loses vital ingredients rapidly. Because so little soil is involved, only a diluted form of fertilizer should be used. This means diluting a house plant fertilizer or fish emulsion at the rate of half or a quarter of what the manufacturer indicates. Make it a quarter for plants in pots without drainage holes, since fertilizer salts have no way of flushing out and therefore can accumulate. If directions say one tablespoon per gallon of water, make it one half or one quarter of a tablespoon. Since a gallon—the frequent formula given by manufacturers—would fertilize countless dozens of midget gardens, brush up on your math and make just one pint. Store any left over in a covered plastic jar.

Don't fertilize a sickly plant. This won't bring it back. The plant needs rest to recover, not a jolt to the system. Avoid fertilizing during dark and rainy days. Don't fertilize and water separately on the same day. Let the fertilized solution replace the scheduled watering.

There are many house plant fertilizers on the market. Some are liquids or powders to be mixed with water; others are tablets to be inserted in the soil. There are also slow-release fertilizers, which act over a period of several months. For very small containers, one has better control over the amount of fertilizer given if it's in liquid form, whether from a concentrate or powder. When just a few drops are needed, only a liquid can be used with any degree of efficiency.

Plants don't need to be fertilized during the winter months. Some go into dormancy; most just keep the status quo. It's when spring comes around and plants begin active growth that they need their "vitamins" every few weeks. Flowering plants do a better job of blooming if they're fertilized. Fertilize every two or three weeks throughout spring and summer; then forget about it until the following year.

Vacation Care

First, let's hear the bad news. Miniature gardens dry out very quickly, so it's not possible to let them fend for themselves, even for a few days. You can, however, use the trick of placing newspapers at the bottom of a sink or bathtub, soaking them thoroughly, and then placing the watered dish garden or pots on top of the damp papers. Cover the plants with clear plastic, the kind you get from the dry cleaners, making sure that it doesn't touch the plants. Use a bent wire coat hanger to keep the plastic away from the plants. Tuck the plastic under the containers to prevent air from getting in. Leave the light on in the room, and you can go away for a week. The larger the pot, the lesser the risk, since more moisture is stored. Obviously, there is no need to do anything with cacti or succulents. They'll be waiting for you when you return just as happy as they were when you left.

Now the good news. Miniature gardens are very portable. Because they're so small, it's easy to carry one or two to a neighbor's or friend's house for safe keeping. Make sure you tell them exactly what your watering routine is so they can duplicate it. You can't cart around a dozen large pots, but it's a cinch to take a few miniatures to somebody else's home, even to your office. Leave one on your desk, and ask a fellow employee to keep an eye on it. Plentiful fluorescent office lighting will keep the plants thriving. If you're a frequent traveler, stick with cacti and succulents.

9.

Plants for
Miniature
Gardens

There are two types of plants that can be used alone or combined to create indoor dish gardens: young standard-sized plants or their seedlings, and genuine miniature plants. Both are equally effective, and I recommend combining them in various arrangements. Each type has advantages and disadvantages. In the case of the young plants, they are readily available at any plant shop or even variety store. However, they have to be pruned to restrict their normal growth. Let too long a period go by, and it's too late to prune the plant so it can still look attractive. A severe crewcut is not indicated; rather, do a gentle, steady trimming. Much depends on the form of the plant. Some can't be trimmed no matter what (such as ferns and palms), although mature growth can be cut back to soil level, leaving only new growth. Fortunately they take a long time to grow, so that it's easy a year or two later to dig up the plant, pot it in its own container, and replace it in the dish garden with another seedling, starting the cycle all over again.

There is no such fuss with real miniatures. They'll never grow beyond their prescribed height. If it's a four-inch plant, it'll still be four inches high after years of growth. No pruning is needed except to perfect the shape. The only disadvantage is that these plants are not easy to come by locally; they must be purchased by mail from nurseries specializing in such varieties, but the rewards are well worth the extra trouble. Do send for their catalogs. You'll see detailed descriptions of each variety with many illustrations in color. *My listing is merely to whet your appetite.* Nurseries specializing in begonias, for instance, list hundreds of varieties, out of which you select the miniatures for your own use. (See pages 131–35 for list of suppliers). Also, miniature plants are more expensive than the seedlings bought at neighborhood stores, but one must realize that many years of costly experimentation are necessary to produce these Lilliputian replicas of regular plants. Their culture requirements are a bit more exacting than the common house plants, which is why I suggest that one acquire some experience with house plants before investing in them. But what a delight when one first admires the unbelievably dainty flower of the miniature sinningia or the tiniest geranium in full bloom!

The listing of plants on the following pages includes the major plant categories needed to get the indoor gardener started. Young plants with tiny leaves are excellent to use as "trees" when the lower leaves are cut off to form the "trunk." Train your eye to look for such seedlings in plant stores. Those with small, bushy growth are fine to use as "shrubs" in the landscape; keep them trimmed to the proper size.

When it comes to notes on culture requirements, it's important to remember that conditions indoors vary greatly from similar ones outdoors. Thus, "full sun" outdoors is far more intense than full sun inside a house, which explains why certain plants that would be normally grown in the shade outdoors can be grown in a sunny spot inside the home. The same holds true of "shade." Except for deep woods or forest, shady areas in the garden do get a certain amount of bright light, if not sun, during the day. Not so in many indoor situations. A "shady" nook in an apartment should really be accurately termed a "dark" corner many times. In addition, sunlight differs according to the seasons. It's at its most intense during the summer months, coming through a south window without any screening such as curtains or blinds. This same location during the winter presents an entirely different environment for plants. It all comes down to using one's own common sense. Follow the instructions given here, but move your little gardens around the room or to another part of the house if you notice that they're not doing so well.

A terrarium, whether open or closed, should never be placed in direct sunlight. Bright light is fine, but direct sun, intensified through the plastic or glass, turns the terrarium into an oven with the plants getting thoroughly cooked.

When it comes to temperatures, most house plants are quite happy in the winter-summer range of the average home, which means anywhere from 65 to 85 degrees Fahrenheit with a dip of ten degrees at night. Some plants can stand greater cold, however, as low as 35 degrees, as long as it's above freezing. A few, such as evergreens, require cold temperatures in the winter, making their cultivation possible only in enclosed porches or a room deliberately kept under 60 degrees. If an evergreen seedling is looked upon as purely a temporary plant in a dish garden, to be replaced when it dies in six months or so, then it can be displayed in a normally heated room, well out of direct sun.

Watering has been covered in Chapter 8, but a few notes are in order to explain the definition of *moist* and *dry.* Most plants go through a dormancy period in late fall and winter, and even though the rest of the year they may require lots of moisture, it's wise to let plants dry out before watering again during their dormancy. Keeping plants on the dry side during the dark days of winter is added protection against diseases and pests. As the plant begins active growth in spring, resume whatever water schedule is necessary (some plants like it dry all the time). So, when the word *moist* appears next to a plant, keep the soil evenly moist during the active growth period but on the drier side during winter. If *dry* is noted, keep the plant dry all year, watering sparingly, once a week or so in summer, much less in winter. Where nothing special is noted next to the plant's name, this refers to the average, the vast majority, of plants grown in pots with drainage holes: water thoroughly, let soil dry out, then water thoroughly again until you see water coming out the bottom holes.

Where *humidity* is mentioned next to a plant, it means that this plant requires above-normal humidity to grow well. Such a plant is ideal for terrariums or grouped with similar humidity-loving plants inside a former fish tank or in a giant brandy snifter. Otherwise, place the plant on a tray filled with pebbles that are kept constantly moist—but don't let water go above the surface of the pebbles. Pots can sit on a bit of water for an hour or so, but any more than this and the roots start to rot. Grouping plants together automatically creates additional humidity, as well as making a pretty decorating touch.

I cannot overemphasize the need for experimentation. Whatever "rules" gardening books stress in their sincere efforts to help us grow beautiful, healthy plants, nothing beats experience. This teaches us that nature is far more flexible than we give her credit for. This is *not* recommended, but I've sometimes combined plants of differing needs in the same container, and to my amazement they've grown very well. Obviously, one or the other had to adapt to a different environment.

My greenhouse is not air-conditioned, and in the summer the temperature inside goes well past 100 degrees, how far past I don't know because that's where the thermometer stops. Since my plants would die in this excessive heat, I take them all out every Memorial Day weekend (except for the cacti and succulents) and place them under trees, around the terrace, hang them from branches, plant them in window boxes—every likely spot is commandeered when you have to find an outdoor home for over four hundred plants. I had no room in the house last summer for the indoor miniature gardens pictured in this book, so I also left them outdoors at the mercy of the elements. I agonized during each downpour, knowing that many of these dish gardens had no drainage holes (not that it would have done them any good even with holes because these tiny gardens are meant for the protective shelter of indoors). Whenever possible, I tipped the small containers over to let excess water drain out, but they still remained very damp from rainfall. However, nothing horrible happened to them. I mention this story only to illustrate that disaster is not always the result of defying the rules.

The numbers 1, 2, and 3 in the list refer to the type of soil mixture that is best for the plant. These mixtures are detailed on page 67. Colors refer to flowers unless otherwise noted.

Also remember that house plants cannot live forever. Even outdoors, in their natural habitat, plants thrive, reproduce, and die. Professional growers, who have the facilities to reproduce as closely as possible the natural environment of specific plants, have losses and expect them. So should you, without developing feelings of guilt or looking at your hands and seeing ten purple thumbs. If you keep losing the same type of plant, don't persist. Obviously your home is not the perfect host for it. Try something else. But don't give up.

I have included spring bulbs in the list of plants because they are such a colorful addition to the indoor garden, coming at a time when one's spirits need a booster shot. These bulbs must be forced to bloom indoors, but the results are rewarding. There are miniature varieties of daffodils, tulips and hyacinths, as well as the regular so-called minor bulbs, such as Snowdrops. Plant them alone in little pots and group them together near a sunny window, or if you wish, you can incorporate them in your indoor landscapes. When you're designing your mini-garden, preferably a woodland scene, place a small empty pot where you'd like to have a few miniature bulbs. Put in the other plants and finish the design. When the "twin" pot with its little bulbs about to burst into bloom is ready, all you do is substitute it for the empty one. Add green moss around and on top of it to hide the pot, and you have a lovely spring landscape. When the blooms have faded, several weeks later, remove the pot and either replace it with a foliage plant or fill in the hole with moss.

Here is how to force these little bulbs. They must be planted in the fall, anytime between September 1 and December 1, depending on how early or late you wish flowers. Place a layer of tiny, broken pieces of clay pots or gravel at the bottom of the pot. Add enough soil (mixture #1) to the container so that when you put the bulbs in, the tips barely reach the rim of the pot. Press bulbs into the soil gently and close enough together so that they are almost touching. The size of the bulbs varies according to the variety, but it's more decorative to have at least three tiny bulbs in each pot.

After planting, pour additional soil between the bulbs, and fill the container to within a half inch of the top. Make sure tips of bulbs are above surface. Water thoroughly. Take pots to an unheated garage, basement, terrace or refrigerator (anywhere between 35 to 48 degrees) and leave them there for twelve weeks, making sure that the soil is kept moist. Apartment dwellers can leave the pots on their terraces, but plants must be kept from freezing. To prevent this, place a layer of mulch on top of the surface and wrap the whole pot in newspapers or styrofoam, placing it as close to the building wall as possible for maximum protection, and anchored against the wind. Regular waterings can be done through the mulch and papers. Do a similar wrap-up job if storing in refrigerator. After twelve weeks, check to see if there are shoots about two inches high, in which case the pots can be brought indoors in a semidark, cool area for further growth. Otherwise, leave the pots where they are for another two weeks. When leaves and buds begin to appear, move the pots to a lighted area or insert them, pot and plant, in one of your mini-gardens as mentioned earlier. Keep watering the plant regularly. It will not force again, so when it has stopped blooming, take the pot out and throw out the plant. Or plant the bulb outdoors the following fall, and maybe, just maybe, it may bloom again the next spring.

Achimenes: Gesneriad. Some tiny varieties, upright or trailing: "Camille Brozzoni," violet/white. "Carmine Queen," red. A. Fimbriata, white. A. flava, yellow. A. pulchella, orange/red. Partial shade or sun. Moist. 65 to 85 degrees F. Humidity. #2. Plant only one rhizome in small container. Keep pinching tips until June.

Acorus gramineus pusillus: Japanese Sweet Flag, dwarf variety. Upright, 3 inches. Swordlike leaves resembling grass. Also grows in water. Acorus gramineus variegatus, 9 inches, green and white striped leaves. Sun. 60 to 85 degrees F. #1.

Aglaonema commutatum maculatum: Silver Evergreen. Upright. Also grows in water or terrarium. Buy young plants. A. modestum, Chinese Evergreen. Sun. Humidity. 60 to 70 degrees F. Moist. #1.

Asplenium platyneuron: Ebony Spleenwort. Miniature rock fern. Terrarium. Shade. 60 to 75 degrees F. Humidity. Moist. #1.

Azalea: Dwarf varieties or keep pruning young plants to keep them under 10 inches. Sun or shade. Keep *under* 60 degrees F. Moist. #2.

Begonia: Large variety of miniatures, upright or trailing, in many colors. Some good mini-Rex: "Baby Rainbow," "Granny," "Lorraine Closson," "Peridot" (the tiniest of all), and "Red Berry." Some Rhizomatous varieties: "China Doll," "Bow-Joe," "Chantilly Lace," B. Prismatocarpa. Good wax varieties: "Andy," "Pied Piper," "Pistachio." The semituberous variety "Foliosa" looks just like a dainty fern. A must in any collection and a fine accent plant in a mini-landscape. Sun or shade. Moist. 60 to 85 degrees F. #2. Also good for open terrarium.

Buxus microphylla compacta: Kingsville Boxwood. Very tiny leaves. Good for "hedges" and "shrubs." Sun or shade. Keep *under* 60 degrees F. #1.

Cacti: Impossible to do a desert scene without cacti, although a handsome cactus by itself in a small, decorative clay pot is a very pleasing sight. Whichever way you choose to use them, you have a mind-boggling selection at your disposal. Start with the varieties available at your local stores, then when you get hooked (and you will) send for the catalogs of specialists in this field. It's a whole new world of gardening. Team cacti with other succulents for maximum effect. While cacti are part of the succulent family, they are in a field by themselves. Sun. 55 to 85 degrees. Dry. #3.

Caladium humboldtii: A miniature version of the beautiful standard-sized caladiums. Not over 8 inches. Green leaves with white markings. There are

other dwarf varieties but they're all larger in size. Sun or shade. 60 to 85 degrees F. Moist. #2.

Calathea micans: Miniature Maranta. Upright. 6 inches. C. roseo-picta (bi-color), 8 inches. Other varieties. They look somewhat like caladiums. Shade. 60 to 85 degrees F. Moist. #2.

Carissa grandiflora: Natal Plum. Buy the dwarf variety, white, fragrant flowers. Superb plant for bonsai training. Sun. 60 to 85 degrees F. #1.

Chlorophytum bichetti: Miniature version of the popular spider plant but without the "spiders" trailing. 4 inches. Also good for terrarium. Sun. 60 to 85 degrees F. Moist. #1.

Codiaeum variegatum pictum: var. "Punctatum aureum." Miniature Croton. Also good for terrarium or in water. Sun. 60 to 85 degrees F. Humidity. #1.

Codonanthe carnosa: A great little miniature for baskets. Small succulent leaves, white bell-shaped flowers and tiny orange berries. Sun. Humidity. Moist. 60 to 85 degrees F. #2.

Cordyline terminalis: "Baby Doll" is a lovely miniature. Sun. 70 to 85 degrees F. #1.

Crassula: Many, many varieties in this succulent family. Thick stems and fleshy leaves. C. argenta is the well-known Jade Plant. Easily kept under control when young, or buy the miniature variety, Aeonium sedifolium. C. lycopodiodes monstrosa is heavily branched with upright stems. C. schmidtii, 3 inches, has fleshy, needlelike leaves and brick-red flowers. C. cooperii is a trailer with small white flowers. The Jade Plant can also grow in water. Sun. 65 to 85 degrees F. Moist. #3.

Cryptanthus: Bromeliad that grows in a low rosette form. Many small varieties, highly colorful. A good accent for a desert scene. Sun. 60 to 75 degrees F. #1 plus 3 parts of osmunda fiber.

Cuphea hyssopifolia: False heather. 5 inches. "Shrub" leaves under ½ inch and violet/white flowers under ¼ inch long. Sun. 65 to 75 degrees. #2.

Cyanotis kewensis: (Brown teddy bear). Trailing

with hairy stems and leaves. Blue or violet flowers. Sun. 60 to 85 degrees. F. #1.

Cyperus alternifolius gracilis: Dwarf Umbrella Plant. Good as a "tree." Regular-sized plant can also be used this way if bought very young. Sun or shade. 65 to 85 degrees F. #1.

Dracaena godseffiana: Green leaves spotted with white markings. Very slow growing so that it's good to use as "trees" when bought young. Also suitable for terrariums. D. terminalis "Baby Doll" sometimes called Cordyline terminalis is also effective. Sun or shade. 60 to 85 degrees F. Moist. #1.

Echeverria: A large genus of tropical succulent plants. Thick leaves growing in rosette form. E. derenbergii is a small variety but there are others listed by specialists. Sun. 65 to 85 degrees F. Moist. #1.

Episcia: Leaves are as beautiful as the flowers. Highly prized plants of the gesneriad family. Tiny varieties: "Emerald Green," "Jenny Elbert," and the trailing E. dianthiflora. Shade. 65 to 85 degrees F. Moist. Humidity. #2.

Eunoymus japonica microphyllus: Good as miniature "hedge" or "tree." Sun or shade. 32 to 70 degrees F. #1.

Evergreens: The dwarf varieties listed below vary in size, can be as tiny as a golf ball. Buy young plants anyway, although they grow so slowly you can barely notice it. *Cedrus deodara nana:* Cedar, gray-blue foliage. C. libani sargenti, pendulus branches. *Chamaecyparis obtusa coespitosa:* Dwarf Cypress, no bigger than a golf ball in size and shape. C. pygmaea Chimo-Hiba, flat topped, very tiny. C. nana, blue-green foliage. C. plumosa compressa aurea nana, yellow foliage, cushion shape. *Abies balsamea nana:* Fir, globe shaped. *Thuja occidentalis ellwangeriana nana aurea:* Arbor-vitae, has yellow foliage, pyramidal shape. T. orientalis juniperioides has globular shape, gray in summer, plum-colored in winter. *Pinus densiflora pygmaea:* Pine, very slow-growing, short needles. *Taxus baccata adpressa aurea:* Yew, variegated golden leaves. T. baccata fastigiata

Standishi, pyramidal shape, golden foliage. *Tsuga canadensis cole's prostrate:* Canadian Hemlock, variety with prostrate habit. T. canadensis minima, one of the dwarfest forms. T. diversifolia, dwarf Japanese hemlock. *Dwarf rhododendrons:* Myrtilloides, 6 to 8 inches, purple flowers. Camtschaticum, 4 to 6 inches, purple flowers. Pemakaense, 8 to 10 inches high, pink flowers. Charitophes, 10–12 inches, pink flowers. *Cryptomeria elegans nana,* green leaves turn purple in the fall. C. Pygmaea, hanging branches. *Juniperus communis compressa:* Miniature Irish Juniper, columnar form. J. Scopulorum palmeri, creeping Juniper, blue foliage. J. squamata Meyeri, upright Juniper, very blue. *Picea procumbens:* Spruce, slow growing, prostrate habit. P. pumila, fan-shaped branches, dense habit. For *all* these evergreens: shade or sun, temperature *under* 60 degrees F., which means cool rooms or a cool greenhouse. #2.

Ferns: Buy young plants of regular varieties that will remain small (keep cutting older fronds down to the base to keep them small) or buy miniatures such as Adiantum bellow, Adiantum capillus-veneris, Adiantum hispidulum, and Adiantum raddianum, which are all tiny maidenhair ferns, good also in terrariums, or Polystichumts tsus-simense, a dwarf fern also good for terrariums. Pteris ensiforis "Victoriae" (Silver table fern) is a very pretty miniature with silver and green fronds. There's also Polypodium vacciniifolium and Nephrolepis exaltata cv. Childsii or cv. Mini-ruffles. Shade. Humidity. Moist. 60 to 70 degrees F. #2. Some other ferns have adapted to dry climate such as Actiniopteris, Cheilanthes, and Pellaea. These also can be cut down to size very easily.

Fittonia verschaffeltii or *F. argyoneura:* both not over 8 inches high with colorful leaves. Spreading habit makes them suitable ground covers. Also good for terrariums. Shade. Humidity. 60 to 85 degrees F. Moist. #2.

Geraniums: There are now many beautiful varieties of miniature geraniums all between 6 and 8 inches high. To give you just a few names: "Pompeii," double, red. "Sugar Baby" an ivy leaf miniature with pink flowers. "Fleurette," a double coral. "Altair," double orange/pinkish red. "Venus," a light pink. "Lyric" is lavender. "Little Darling," another lovely pink. "Pigmy" is a double red. "Imp," a dark salmon. "Ruffles" naturally has ruffled salmon flowers while "Tiny Tim" is red. Sun. 55 to 70 degrees. Keep on the dry side during winter months, giving more water during spring and summer. #1.

Haworthia: Many dwarf varieties of this unusual succulent. Thick, fleshy pointed leaves that grow in a sort of rosette pattern. Partial sun. 55 to 75 degrees F. Dry in winter, moist in summer. #3.

Hedera helix: English ivy. Some have very tiny leaves, others are true miniatures. Many uses in the dish garden. Cut off the lower leaves and they become "trees," prune back and they're "shrubs" or background greenery. Also grow in water. Some small-leaved varieties: "Gold Heart," "Irish Lace," and "Merion Beauty." Miniatures: "Triloba," "Walthamensis," "Jubilee," and "Glacier." Shade/partial sun. Moist. 40 to 70 degrees F. #2.

Helxine soleilroli: Baby's-tears. H. nana, dwarf baby's tears. Excellent as a ground cover. Leaves are so tiny and green, the effect is that of moss. Use manicuring scissors to keep in bounds. Also good for terrariums. Shade/sun. 35 to 85 degrees F. Humidity. Moist. #1.

Hoya minima: Dwarf hoya. Tiny, round, dark green leaves with pink flowers. Use whenever a trailing plant is needed to hang from edge of container. H. bella is a shrubby plant with branches that first go upright, then hang down. Especially good for baskets. White flowers with purple center. H. lucunosa has olive green leaves with fragrant greenish-yellow flowers. Sun. 60 to 85 degrees F. #2.

Impatiens: Buy dwarf varieties that come in several colors. Shade or partial sun. 60 to 85 degrees F. Moist. Humidity. #1.

Jasminum: Jasmine. Several varieties, upright or trailing. Buy young plants and use them as "trees." The trailing variety stands upright when young and

kept cut down. Sun. 35 to 70 degrees F. Humidity. #1.

Kalanchoe: Tiny-flowered succulents. K. blossfeldiana, dwarf under 8 inches with red flowers. K. blossfeldiana "Tom Thumb," under 6 inches, comes with yellow or red flowers. Sun. 60 to 85 degrees F. #1.

Koellikeria erinoides: Leaves grow flat in rosette form, with spray-type flowers. Sun. 60 to 85 degrees F. Moist. #2.

Lycopodium lucidulum: Evergreen Club Moss. Upright stems. Good to use as "trees." Requires exceptionally high humidity, so use in terrariums only. Shade. Moist. Humidity. 30 to 75 degrees F. #2.

Malpighia coccigera: One of my all-time favorite plants. Resembles a dwarf holly but actually comes from the Caribbean. Grows very, very slowly. Excellent for bonsai training. Six or eight tiny rooted cuttings from the plant make a wonderful holly "forest" when grouped together in a dish garden. If you're lucky, you may also get lots of dainty pink starlike flowers. A real gem of a plant. Sun. 60 to 85 degrees F. Moist. #2.

Mentha requienii: Corsican mint. It resembles but is smaller than baby's tears and fragrant—of mint, naturally. Excellent to use as a ground cover for bonsai, terrariums, or woodland scenes. Shade. Moist. Humidity. #1 or #2.

Monanthes polyphylla: A dwarf variety of the hen-and-chicks succulent. Only ½ inch high. M. muralis is a 3-inch miniature succulent with a bonsai look about it. Sun. Moist only during summer. 50 to 85 degrees F. #3.

Orchids: There are many beautiful miniatures in this fascinating family of plants. They take several months to adjust to a new environment, so patience is necessary. Sun or shade, depending on the variety. Water once a week, keep temperature around 75 degrees F. Best bet: follow specialist nurseryman's instructions that come with each orchid. Plant each orchid by itself. Terrestrial orchids like regular humus-rich soil, or plain peat moss, or chopped osmunda with loam (soil) and sphagnum moss. Epiphytic orchids (get their food from air) are planted in osmunda or fir bark. Some even grow happily merely attached to slabs of osmunda or tree fern fiber. Provide the high humidity they require by grouping them inside an open terrarium or a large brandy snifter or on a tray covered with moist pebbles. Some recommended varieties: Cattleya luteola, 6–7 inches, pale yellow. Dendobrium linguiforme, 4 inches, white. Epidendrum mariae, 6 inches, green/white. Dendrobium aggregatum, 8 inches, yellow, fragrant. Laelia pumila, 8 inches, rose/yellow. Odontoglossum-pulchellum, 8 inches, white, fragrant. Oncidium cheirophorum, 6 inches, fragrant, yellow/green. Pleurothallis picta, 2 inches, orange. Ornithocephalus bicornis, 2 inches, greenish/white. Dendrobium jenkinsii, 2 inches, yellow. Miniature Cymbidiums need cool, airy locations.

Oxalis hedysaroides rubra: Wood Sorrel. Keep young plant under 6 inches and use it as a "tree." Also good for open terrarium. O. lobata is 3 inches high, stemless with yellow flowers. Shade or sun. 60 to 75 degrees F. Moist. Humidity. #1 or #2.

Palms: Very young plants are good for tropical dish gardens. Cut old stems at base to control size. Two of the best are the popularly called Neanthe bella (its correct name is Chamaedorea elegans or Collinia elegans), and the Areca palm or cane palm (Chrysalidocarpus lutescens). 65 to 85 degrees F. Moist. Humidity. #1.

Peperomia: Many, many varieties. Use as "shrubs" when young such as P. glabella or P. acuminata. P. caperata tricolor is an upright miniature. P. prostrata is trailing. Shade. 60 to 85 degrees. Humidity. #2.

Philodendron oxycardium (sodiroi): Buy only as a young plant. Good grown in water or in a terrarium as well. Shade. 60 to 85 degrees. #1.

Phinaea multiflora: Plant only one rhizome or several if a drift of tiny, white-flowered plants is desired. Also good in terrariums. Part sun. Humidity. Moist. #2.

Pilea depressa: A 1-inch high, trailing, ground cover. Buy young plants and keep pruning to size. Several varieties. P. cadieri minima is the miniature Aluminum Plant, under 6 inches. P. nummularifolia (Creeping Charlie) trails or hangs as you wish. A good ground cover. Use P. muscosa as a "tree." Sun or shade. 60 to 85 degrees F. Moist. Humidity. #1 or #2.

Podocarpus alpinus: P. macrophyllus Maki. Buy young plants to use as "trees." Sun. 32 to 72 degrees F. #2.

Roses: Each year the list of miniature roses grows more impressive. Grow these little gems alone in pretty pots or, in the larger indoor garden, as a "regular" rose bush. Choose from miniature tea, floribunda, and moss varieties. Just a few hints: "Cinderella," white. "Tiny Flame," "Red Imp," "Pink Ribbon," "Yellow Bantam," "Lavender Lace," "Jeanie Williams," blends. "Chipper," pink. "Toy Clown," blends. "Kara," pink. "Magic Carousel," blends. "Yellow Doll." "Beauty Secret," red. "Scarlet Gem." Sun. Humidity. 50 to 85 degrees F. #2.

Saintpaulia: African violets. Impossible to name all the many lovely miniature varieties which come in single or double flowers and in so many colors. They're all under 6 inches in diameter. Simply choose your favorites from this dazzling collection. Although they blend well in some mini-landscapes, I prefer using them alone in unusual containers. Also good for open terrariums. Any window exposure will do, except in the summer when a south window becomes too bright unless you draw blinds across it or have glass curtains. 60 to 85 degrees F. Humidity. Moist. #2 or buy the already packaged soil made especially for African violets.

Sansevieria "hahnii": Dwarf birdsnest sansevieria. Comes in handy when sharp, swordlike leaves are needed as a background accent in a dish garden. Adds variety to indoor landscaping. Shade. 60 to 85 degrees F. #1.

Saxifraga sarmentosa: Strawberry geranium. There are several varieties. Grow one in a regular

pot, and plant one of the "babies" it sends out in the dish garden. When the "baby" (offshoot of the plant, which like the Spider Plant, is a tiny, dangling replica of the mother plant) grows too large, replace it with another one and so on. One plant will not only keep you supplied for ages, but your friends as well. Partial shade or sun. 35 to 75 degrees F. Humidity. #1.

Scindapsis pictus argyraens: Pothos. Buy the young plant only. Also good growing in water or in a terrarium. Shade. 60 to 85 degrees F. Humidity. #2.

Sedum: Stonecrop. Over 500 species alone! Low growing, creeping varieties or upright. Invaluable in doing mini-gardens not only for desert landscapes but because they are so undemanding as to culture. Just a few favorites: S. morganianum (Donkey's tail) hangs, what else? S. multiceps (Pigmy Joshua Tree), 6 inches, a miniature branched tree with tiny rosette leaves and yellow flowers. S. dasyphyllum, a sprawler, matted blue-gray foliage in tiny rosette, white flowers. S. lineare, creeping, good for terrariums too, greenish-gray leaves with white margins. S. humifusum, trailing stems, stays tiny. Sun. Water during active growth, then very little. 35 to 85 degrees F. #3.

Selaginella uncinata: Rainbow Club Moss. S. kraussiana brownii, "Irish Moss." Excellent as ground cover, as accent, or in terrarium. Shade. 35 to 85 degrees F. Moist. Humidity. #2.

Sinningia pusilla: Superlatives are reserved for this little beauty. Give it high, high humidity, in a terrarium preferably, and marvel at how this minuscule plant keeps on blooming. A must for the woodland scene when "wild flowers" are desired. Some jewels: "Doll Baby," "Poupee," "Wood Nymph," "Bright Eyes," "White Sprite," S. concinna. Moist. Humidity. Semishade. 65 to 85 degrees F. #2.

Spring bulbs: Must all be forced. See page 115 for instructions. Excellent *Daffodil* miniatures: Narcissus Bulbocodium obesus, 5 inches, yellow. N. Watieri, 4 inches, white. N. Juncifolius, 5 inches, yellow. N.

Lady Bee, 5 inches, white/pink. *Galanthus:* Snow-drops. G. nivalis, 6 inches, has single white flowers. G. nivalis flore pleno is also 6 inches and has double white flowers. *Hyacinths:* Dwarf varieties include "Rosalie," a pink, and "Vanguard," which is light blue. *Muscari:* Grape hyacinths. M. azureum album (5″) is white; M. azureum (6″) is blue. *Puschkinia:* Lebanon Squill, under 5 inches. *Tulips:* Good small varieties: Tulipa batalinii (Botanical species), 6 inches, primrose-yellow. T. linifolia (Botanical), 6 inches, scarlet. T. "Gaiety" (Kaufmanniana species), 4 inches, white inside with pinkish red outer petals. T. Tarda (Dasystemon), 4 inches, bunch-flowering, 3 to 6 flowers per stem, canary-yellow or white with orange-yellow center.

Streptocarpus: "Blue Streaker" is making news as a new miniature hybrid using the species S. cyanandrus and S. rimicola. There's also "Mini-Nympth," "Netta Nymph," S. stomandrus, among others. Also good for terrariums. Sun. Moist. Humidity. 60 to 85 degrees F. #2.

Syngonium podophyllum: Arrowhead plant. Good as "shrubs" when young. Will also grow in water and in terrariums. Shade. 60 to 85 degrees F. Moist. Humidity. #1.

Tradescantia: Wandering Jew. Several miniature varieties available. Good for tiny baskets as well as to grow in water. Shade or sun. 60 to 85 degrees F. #1.

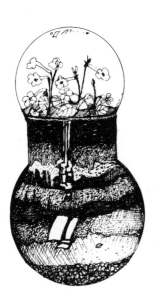

List of Suppliers

List of Suppliers

Abbey Garden
176 Toro Canyon Road
Carpinteria, Calif. 93013

Cacti and succulents

Alberts and Merkel Bros. Inc.
2210 S. Federal Highway
Boynton Beach, Fla. 33435

Miniature orchids
Catalog, 50¢

Alpenglow Gardens
13328 King George Highway
Surrey, D.C. V3T236 Canada

Alpine plants, evergreens

Annalee Violetry
29–50 214th Place
Bayside, N.Y. 11360

Miniature African violets

Armstrong Associates, Inc.
Box 54
Kennebunk, Me. 04043

Carnivorous plants

Barrington Greenhouses
860 Clemente Road
Barrington, N.J. 08016

Miniature house plants

Adam Brentwood
8 Dorothy Avenue
Paramus, N.J. 07652

Terrarium and bonsai plants and supplies
Catalog, 25¢

Buell's Greenhouses
P. O. Box 218, Weeks Road
Eastford, Conn. 06242

Miniature African violets, gloxinias and other gesneriads
Catalog, $1.00

W. Atlee Burpee Co.
300 Park Avenue
Warminster, Pa. 18974

Seeds, supplies including
Viterra Hydrogel

Cactus Gem Nursery
10092 Mann Drive
Cupertino, Calif. 95014

Cacti and succulents

Carroll Gardens
Westminster, Md. 21157

Dwarf evergreens

Cooks Geranium Nursery
712 No. Grand
Lyons, Kansas 67554

Miniature geraniums
Catalog, 35¢

Corliss Bros. Nursery
Essex Road
Ipswich, Mass. 01938

Dwarf evergreens

Davis Cactus Garden
1522 Jefferson Street
Kerrville, Texas 78028

Cacti and succulents

Desert Plant Co.
P. O. Box 889
Marfa, Texas 79843

Cacti and succulents
Catalog, $1.00

Arthur Eames Allgrove
North Wilmington, Mass. 01187

Terrarium and bonsai plants
and supplies
Catalog, 50¢

Eastern Shores Nurseries, Inc.
P. O. Box 743
Easton, Md. 21601

Dwarf evergreens

Edelweiss Gardens
Robbinsville, N.J. 08691

Bonsai plants and others
Catalog, 35¢

Federal Smallwares Corp.
85 Fifth Avenue
New York, N.Y. 10003

Free catalog of their
enormous collections of
miniature furnishings

Fennell Orchid Co.
26715 S.W. 157th Avenue
Homestead, Fla. 33030

Miniature orchids
Catalog, $1.00

Girard Nurseries
P. O. Box 428
Geneva, Ohio 44041

Dwarf evergreens

The Greenhouse
9515 Flower Street
Bellflower, Calif. 90706

Supplies for artificial lighting

House Plant Corner
P. O. Box 810
Oxford, Md. 21654

All kinds of supplies
Catalog, 25¢

Margaret Ilgenfritz Orchids
Box 665
Monroe, Mich. 48161

Miniature orchids
Catalog, $2.00

J & L Orchids
Easton, Conn. 06425

Miniature orchids

P. de Jager and Sons, Inc.
188 Ashbury Street
South Hamilton, Mass. 01982

Bulbs

Jones and Scully Orchids
2200 N.W. 33rd Avenue
Miami, Fla. 33142

Miniature orchids
Catalog, $3.50

Michael J. Kartuz
92 Chestnut Street
Wilmington, Mass. 01887

Assorted miniature plants

Lauray of Salisbury
Undermountain Road
Salisbury, Conn. 06068

Miniature gesneriads
Catalog, 35¢

Logee's Greenhouses
Danielson, Conn. 06239

Miniature begonias and
many other house plants
Catalog, $1.00

Lyndon Lyons Greenhouses
14 Mutchler Street
Dolgeville, N.Y. 13329

Gesneriads—miniatures

Merry Gardens
Camden, Me. 04843

Miniature begonias and others

Mini-Roses
P. O. Box 245 Station A
Dallas, Texas 75208

Miniature roses

Miniature Gazette, N.A.M.E.
Box 2621
Brookhurst Center
Anaheim, Calif. 92804

Quarterly publication of
the National Association
of Miniature Enthusiasts
Annual subscription, $10.00
includes dues

Mott Miniatures
P. O. Box 5514
Sunny Hills Station
Fullerton, Calif. 92635

Quarterly periodical
on miniature furnishings
Annual subscription, $7.00

Nichols Garden Nursery
1190 Pacific Highway
Albany, Ore. 97321

Herbs
Catalog, 25¢

Nor'East Miniature Roses
58 Hammond Street
Rowley, Mass. 01969

Miniature roses

Nutshell News
1035 Newkirk Drive
La Jolla, Calif. 92037

Quarterly publication
on miniature furnishings
Annual subscription, $5.00

Oliver Nurseries
1159 Bronson Road
Fairfield, Conn. 06430

Dwarf evergreens

George W. Park Seed Co., Inc. Greenwood, S.C. 29647	Seeds and supplies
Peter Pauls Nurseries Rye, 4 Canadaigua, N.Y. 14424	Carnivorous plants
Pixie Treasures 4121 Prospect Avenue Yorba Linda, Calif. 92686	Miniature roses
Plaza Nursery 7430 Crescent Avenue Buena Park, Calif. 90620	Bromeliads
San Francisco Plant Co. P. O. Box 1835 Burlingame, Calif. 94010	Miniature African violets and supplies
Shoplite Co. 566 Franklin Avenue Nutley, N.J. 07110	Everything that's needed for artificial lighting
Sequoia Nursery 2519 East Nobel Street Visalia, Calif. 93277	Miniature roses of all types
Sky-Cleft Gardens Camp Street Extension Barre, Vt. 05641	Alpine plants
Three Springs Fisheries Lilypons, Md. 21717	Miniature waterlilies Catalog, 50¢
Tinari Greenhouses 2325 Valley Road Huntington Valley, Pa. 19006	Miniature African violets Catalog, 25¢
Trifles & Treasures Box 543 Carlsbad, Calif. 92008	Unusual mini-planters

Wilson Bros. Floral Co., Inc. Dwarf geraniums
Roachdale, Ind. 46172

Bibliography

Bibliography

Atkinson, Robert E. *Spot Gardens: A Guide for Creating and Planting Miniature Gardens, Indoors and Outdoors.* New York, McKay. $9.95.

Bagust, Harold. *Miniature Geraniums.* Newton Center, Mass., Branford. $4.25.

Brooklyn Botanic Garden. *Miniature Gardens.* Brooklyn, N.Y. $1.50.*

————. *Japanese Gardens and Miniature Landscapes.* Brooklyn, N.Y. $1.50.*

Ishimoto, Tatsuo. *Art of Growing Miniature Trees, Plants and Landscapes.* New York, Crown. $4.50.

Kawamoto, Toshio. *Saikei: Living Landscapes in Miniatures.* Scranton, Pa., Harper and Row. $8.95.

Kramer, Jack. *Miniature Gardens in Bowl, Dish and Tray.* New York, Scribner. $6.95.

————. *Miniature Plants, Indoors and Out.* New York, Scribner. $6.95, paperback $4.95.

McDonald, Elvin. *Little Plants for Small Places.* New York, M. Evans, and Popular Library. $7.95, paperback $1.50.

Pinney, Margaret E. *Miniature Rosebook for Outdoor and Indoor Culture.* Princeton, N.J., Van Nostrand. Out of print, but so good that if one has the time to hunt around for it, it's well worth it.

Sunset Editors. *Terrariums and Miniature Gardens.* Menlo Park, Calif. $2.45.*

* These excellent handbooks are available at most good local garden centers.

Index